Cecilia Norman was born in Chelsea, London and studied domestic science. After marriage and raising her two daughters she returned to teaching as a home economics teacher in secondary and further education. For several years she taught Recipe Development and the Preparation of Food for Photography to final year students at both The Polytechnic of North London and Croydon College. She is an expert in all forms of cookery and is the Principal of the Microwave Cooking School in Hampstead. She takes an active interest in the Institute of Home Economics and the British Standards Institution. She has written many books, among which *Barbecue Cookery*, *Pancakes and Pizzas*, *The Pie and Pastry Cookbook* and her *Microwave Cookery Course* are also available in Panther Books.

G000270605

By the same author

Microwave Cookery for the Housewife
The Heartwatcher's Cook Book
The Colour Book of Microwave Cooking
Freezer to Microwave Cookery
The Crepe and Pancake Cookbook (re-titled *Pancake and Pizzas* for paperback)
Microwave Cooking
The Sociable Slimmer's Cookbook
Microwave with Magimix
Microwave Cookery Course
The Pie and Pastry Cook Book
Barbecue Cookery

CECILIA NORMAN'S

Food Processor Cookbook

PANTHER
Granada Publishing

Panther Books
Granada Publishing Ltd
8 Grafton Street, London W1X 3LA

Published by Panther Books 1984

Copyright © Cecilia Norman 1984

ISBN 0-586-06341-2

Printed and bound in Great Britain by
Collins, Glasgow

Set in Times

Contents

Acknowledgements

I would like to thank my faithful band of tasters who were compelled to sample about ten recipes a day, including food that did not particularly appeal to them; Claudette McIntosh, the Home Economist, who prepared and cooked the dishes; Inma Teruel who for several months gave up her *au pair* duties to concentrate on recipe checking; my students Mesdames Cannell, Eilon, Robertson and McEwan for particular assistance with the Raspberry Curd recipe; my husband Laurie for putting the book together; and Ian Paten for being such a 'get-on-withable' Editor.

My thanks also to the manufacturers who provided the food processors, enabling me to work out the recipes on a variety of models. In this respect I am indebted to Nik Handley (Iona), Andy King (Thorn), Jane Massey and Jenny Naylor (Moulinex), Tessa Hayward (Magimix), Wendy Braverman (Toshiba), Howard March (Braun), Lynsey Elliot (P.R. for Breville) and Shelley Byfield-Riches of Lesley Bishop (P.R. for Prestige).

Finally my thanks to Alison Baldock and Victoria Lloyd-Davies of the Mushroom Growers Association for supplying morning-fresh mushrooms which slice so well in the food processor.

Introduction

Do I need a food processor if I already have a mixer or a blender? The answer is an emphatic 'Yes'. Although the food processor can carry out many of the processes of the other two, it provides a much fuller service and also has attributes of its own. Not until I was given a food processor as a present did I realize just how useful it is, and now it is an indispensable part of my kitchen equipment. Cooking is the major part of my life – I do it for business and I do it for pleasure, and it gives me most pleasure when I can rely on modern tools whether I am cooking an old-fashioned dish or convenience foods.

The food processor is invaluable because it will not only mix and blend but also chop, grate, slice, purée, cream, beat, sift, and knead. I always found mincing raw meat tedious because the mincer would clog and it was an unpleasant messy business. It was extremely difficult to wash up and food lodged in the discs had to be poked out. This does not happen with the food processor and the results are just as good.

Previously while endeavouring to do a professional job of chopping with the aid of a sharp knife and a board, bits and pieces of food scattered over the floor. Probably I was not sufficiently adept, but chopping in the processor means that all the food is retained in the bowl. Another bonus is that I do not chop chunks out of my fingers any more.

I now rarely have arduously to push unwilling pulps through a sieve, and every last piece of cheese can be grated without leaving a misshapen slice.

The bowl comes with the machine so that I don't have to search out bowls to mix in. All processes are carried out in the same bowl and the few attachments are easy to wash up,

It occurred to me that I would have to clear some storage

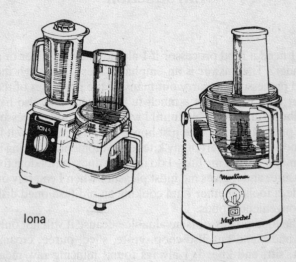

Iona

Moulinex Masterchef

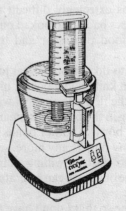

Breville Cyclonic

Braun

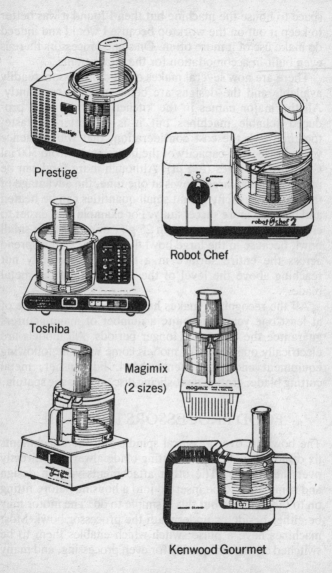

Prestige

Robot Chef

Toshiba

Magimix
(2 sizes)

Kenwood Gourmet

space to house the machine but then I found it was better to keep it out on the worktop because I would and indeed do make use of it more often. On some processors there is even built-in accomodation for the attachments.

There are now several makes of food processors readily available and the designs are being updated constantly. All the major names in the kitchen industry have produced reliable machines but it is a matter of taste, together with the cost consideration, that will influence your choice. The capacity of the bowls varies from 300 ml (½ pt) to 1.5 litres (2½ pt). Although more food can be prepared in the larger bowls at one time, the advantage of the smaller capacity is that small quantities can be beaten and blended more successfully. For example, it is easier to cream 25 g (1 oz) butter with 25 g (1 oz) sugar in a small bowl, because in the large bowl the mixture would spread across the entire surface in a thin layer, possibly not reaching above the level of the upper part of the metal blade.

All the recognized makes have an overall guarantee of at least one year, and quite a number of manufacturers guarantee the motor for longer periods. All models are electrically operated. All models come with the following equipment and attachments: bowl, lid, pusher, metal cutting blade, grating disc, slicing disc, and plastic spatula.

FOOD PROCESSORS IN DETAIL

The bowl fits over a central spindle and the attachments fix on to this. The metal cutting blade always fits directly over the spindle. The other attachments vary in design and some have to be inserted into a housing before fitting on to the machine but this is simple to do. The motor may be either beside or underneath the processor bowl. Most machines have a pulse switch which enables them to be switched on and off quickly for even processing, and many can be operated by a turn of the lid, either clockwise or anti-clockwise, which when clicked into and out of position starts and stops the motor. A pusher is supplied to press the food through the feed tube in the lid, and you should never try to do this with your fingers for obvious reasons. Nearly all food processes can be achieved using the basic attachments.

The bowl Invariably this is shaped like a savarin bowl with a perpendicular tube in the middle – some have rounder sides than others, some have a pouring lip, some a handle and others are ridged inside. They vary in capacity.

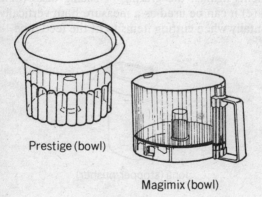

Prestige (bowl)

Magimix (bowl)

The lid The machine cannot be operated unless the lid is in position. This is an excellent safety factor and also prevents the food from spattering. The feed tube is moulded into the lid and one of the models is fitted with a chute enabling sliced food to be ejected into a mixing bowl.

Braun (lid)

The pusher   The pusher is usually made of plastic and sits neatly into the feed tube, a rim preventing it from disappearing into the tube. The pusher has three uses: (a) it prevents food spattering; (b) it holds and presses the ingredients against the grating or slicing discs (or other discs); (c) it can be used as a measure both vertically and horizontally when cutting items to fit the feed tube.

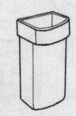

Iona (stopper/pusher)

BASIC ATTACHMENTS
Select the attachment that is best for the job.

Metal Cutting Blade   The metal cutting blade is a double-bladed knife centrally pivoted which, when fixed into position with the machine switched on, revolves at tremendous speed, cutting through the ingredients.

Breville (cutting blade)

Grating Disc   The average grating disc will grate or shred all but the very hardest items.

Slicing Disc   The slicing disc will cope with nearly every food item, but do not use it for ice cubes because it would jam and the cutting edge would be damaged (some *graters* can be used for shaving ice). When only one size of aperture is available, the thickness of the slices can often be regulated by the amount of pressure applied to the pusher.

Kenwood (spatula)

Plastic Spatula   The plastic spatula is intended for scraping down the sides of the bowl during processing. It is also useful for scraping the flat sides of the metal or plastic blades and removing every last particle of mixture from the bowl.

Most preparation can be done with the three basic pieces supplied. For example, you can obtain thicker and thinner slices by adjusting the amount of pressure applied on the pusher, i.e. gentle pressure produces thicker slices.

Grating and shredding discs come in various grades, but if you have only one gauge which may be too fine or too coarse for some processes, the metal blade will substitute. Just process for a little longer, using the pulse switch or lid. Another method of shredding is by first slicing in the food processor, then switching attachments and chopping briefly using the metal blade. To achieve matchsticks or julienne strips, first slice horizontally, then stack the slices together vertically and process once more. It is nice to have a juicer (see optional attachments below) particularly if you want to squeeze several oranges or lemons, although most of us have a lemon squeezer for a single fruit. However, the same function can be performed by chopping the fruit with the metal blade, then straining through a sieve.

If you wish to have a greater choice of thickness of slice or coarseness of shred, purchase a machine which has additional accessories.

OPTIONAL ATTACHMENTS
There are a number of optional attachments available with some machines.
Fine Grating Disc Use for grating hard cheese or crushing ice. It is not suitable for soft, wet items which would clog the tiny holes.

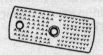

Toshiba (grater)

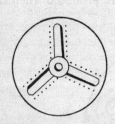

Toshiba (grating disc)

Medium or Coarse Grating Discs Use the medium disc for grating chocolate, ginger root, cheese, etc. Use the coarse disc for salad vegetables such as carrots, celeriac and beetroot or for cabbage.

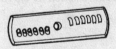

Prestige
(medium/coarse grater)

Magimix
(medium/coarse grater)

Julienne Disc Use for making julienne strips or for coarse grating (the strips are always curved and not similar to the matchstick shapes that are produced when cut by hand).

Julienne (Magimix)

Chipper Disc As its name suggests, use for chipping potatoes. It is also good for chipping other vegetables to be used in salads such as carrots or beetroot.

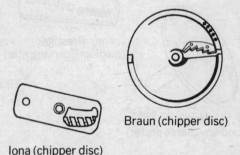

Braun (chipper disc)

Iona (chipper disc)

Thin-Slicing Disc Use for slicing cucumber, potatoes for crisps, or thinly slicing hard cheese such as Cheddar, and chilled cooked meat.

Magimix (thin slicer)

Medium-Slicing Disc Use for slicing celery, firm tomatoes and firm fruit, and chilled raw meat.

Magimix (medium slicer)

Thick-Slicing Disc Use for slicing vegetables to be used in soups or casseroles.

Magimix (thick slicer)

Ripple Disc This is intended to produce slices with a rippled texture suitable for garnishing.

Magimix (ripple disc)

Orange or Lemon Juicer Useful when a large number of fruit are being juiced (take care that you do not hurt your hands while holding the fruit against the dome). When juicing lemons, it is best to cut a slice from the top and then juice the remainder of the lemon rather than cutting in half horizontally as is normal when done manually.

Magimix (citrus press)

Whisk Very good for general whisking purposes but, in my opinion, will not incorporate sufficient air to produce a good meringue. Can be used to thicken cream and whisk light sponge mixes.

Moulinex (whisk)

Plastic Blade This is intended for mixing ingredients where cutting would spoil the texture.

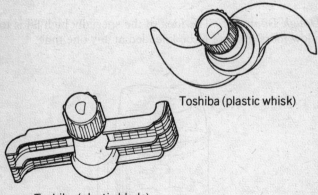

Toshiba (plastic whisk)

Toshiba (plastic blade)

Juice Extractor   The juice extractor is intended to extract juice from vegetables as well as fruit but takes some getting used to.

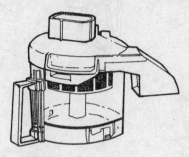

Magimix (juice extractor)

Dough Dome Kit   The idea of the specially high lid is to allow more mixture to be kneaded at any one time.

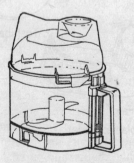

Magimix (dough dome)

Storage Racks and Boxes for Discs   The racks can be easily attached by two screws to the inside of the kitchen cupboard. The boxes will hold the main attachments tidily and also keep out the dust.

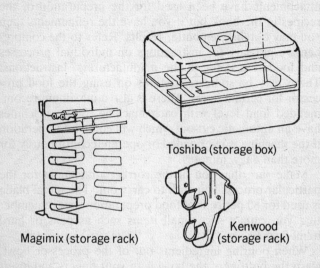

Toshiba (storage box)

Magimix (storage rack)

Kenwood (storage rack)

CARING FOR YOUR FOOD PROCESSOR

Most attachments, the lid and the bowl can be washed in the dishwasher, but be warned – not all are dishwasher-proof, so be guided by the manufacturer's recommendations. Take care when washing and handling the cutting blades and discs as they are very sharp. When washing the grating discs use a brush or soft sponge. Make sure that the bowl and attachments are dried thoroughly before processing dry ingredients, and purchase or make a plastic cover for your machine if it is not in frequent use. The main body of the machine must never be immersed in water.

USING YOUR FOOD PROCESSOR

The food processor can be used to speed and increase efficiency in nearly all food preparation. Only the basic attachments have been used for the preparation of the recipes in the book but if you have the refinements then you may obtain even better results. Refer to the comprehensive glossary for instructions on individual processes and foods but defer to the manufacturers' instructions. There may be some restrictions on using the food processor for certain items. There is also a maximum recommended load level with each machine. Some machines have an automatic cut-out which will come into operation if the machine is overloaded or operated continuously for more than a few minutes.

Make sure that you fit the correct attachment for the particular process you wish to carry out. The metal blade is used for 80 per cent of food preparation, but remember that you cannot slice small items such as peas or hard items such as ice.

When pouring ingredients out of the processor bowl, clasp the bottom of the bowl with your fingers and insert the middle finger into the hole in the centre of the metal blade spigot, pressing firmly towards one side, with a finger of the other hand steadying the top of the metal blade. The blade will then stay in place instead of dropping into the poured-out mixture. (This will not work on all models.)

Use *either* the metric *or* the Imperial measurements given but do not attempt to mix Imperial and metric in one recipe. All the spoon measures given are *level* spoons. For most recipes margarine or butter are suitable. Soft margarine can be used in recipes calling for softened butter.

Take time to study the manufacturers' instructions printed in the booklet that comes with the machine.

Fitting the processor lid is sometimes tricky and you must practise switching on and off rapidly as this could make a big difference to your finished result. Some machines have a choice of speeds. On single-speed machines or maximum power the food processor operates rapidly. Over-processing will turn chopped food into purée in seconds.

HOW TO USE THIS BOOK

The glossary of techniques is intended to guide you when you are uncertain about which attachment to use or how to carry out a particular process. Refer to this section whenever you need to know how to prepare ingredients in the best possible way for all your favourite recipes.

Turn to the all-in-one recipe section for easy-to-prepare recipes which should require little or no practice.

Each stage in the step-by-step recipes is set out in chronological order so that you will know exactly where you were should you be interrupted while cooking.

The combination recipes are mostly made up of a selection of processed ingredients which can be prepared in advance.

In the fast food chapter I make use of frozen and convenience foods and hasten the cooking with the use of the pressure cooker or the microwave oven, but the recipes may be prepared by conventional means if you prefer.

At the back of the book you will find a list of manufacturers should you need any further advice.

A Glossary of Food Processing Techniques

Keep your food processor assembled and ready for use, in an easily accessible place – preferably near to your working area – and you will find yourself using it for most of the jobs that you would otherwise do by hand. If your food processor is tidily stowed away you will not be using it to the full, finding the constant lifting and carrying too much of a bother. You have acquired the food processor to work for you and not the other way round – and be assured that it will perform brilliantly.

This comprehensive glossary is intended as a guide to show you how to prepare the ingredients for all kinds of cooking. Most ingredients can be prepared well in advance ready for the moment when you want to use them.

To obtain the best results:

(1) Never overload the food processor bowl.
(2) Wet mixtures should never reach beyond the top of the spindle or they will overflow into the mechanism.
(3) When using the shredding or slicing discs an overload will cause soft foods to mash as they are pressed down, and the discs will cease to operate properly if food is jammed up against them from underneath.
(4) When using the metal blade uneven chopping is usually due to placing too much in the bowl at any one time; if you are dealing in larger quantities, it is best to process in smaller lots, removing each portion after it has been sufficiently chopped.
(5) When puréeing do not overfill the processor bowl with liquid, which could be forced between the edges of bowl and lid while processing.

(6) When using the grating or slicing discs and switching off between each 'filling' of the feed tube, several batches of processed ingredients can be left in the processor bowl until it is full.

(7) Before grating or shredding, test a small quantity first in order to make certain you have fitted the correct disc.

(8) When using the slicing discs, always fully engage the lid on the bowl before switching on the machine; this makes it easier to hold the pusher in position for the first few cuts and prevents the first slice from becoming jagged as it is pushed over the cutting blade.

(9) After switching off wait until the blade or disc comes to a standstill before removal, or any bits and pieces lodged between the disc and the lid will shoot out.

(10) Always remove the lid before disengaging the bowl from the base.

(11) To chop evenly with the metal blade switch on and off (pulse) rapidly during processing.

(12) Cut large pieces of food into sizes that will fit snugly into the feed tube – use the pusher as a measure. Leave a small head space at the mouth (top end) of the feed tube so that the pusher can slot in securely.

(13) Position single tall, slender items (such as cucumber) against the inside of the tube furthest away from the direction of the cutting edge of the blade.

(14) Never insert your fingers into the feed tube.

(15) Never drop metal implements into the feed tube.

(16) Always switch off after use.

(17) Do not immerse the working parts in water.

(18) Follow the manufacturer's recommendations for safety and maintenance.

(19) Do not pour boiling liquid into the processor bowl unless there are other ingredients already in the bowl.

(20) Process dry ingredients before wet ones.

(21) Remove the bowl before detaching the blade or disc. Discs will then be easier to remove.

Whatever you do you must always refer to the manufacturer's handbook, because there are various load levels, various lengths of continuous processing time, various recommendations for processing hard items such as ice and coffee beans, and not all manufacturers recommend the use of the dishwasher.

ALMONDS
Metal Blade   *To chop whole unskinned almonds:* Arrange up to 100 g (4 oz) to an even depth in the processor bowl. Insert the pusher in the feed tube. Pulse at 3-second intervals to achieve even-sliced fragments.

Metal Blade   *To chop whole blanched almonds:* Spread on a baking tray and dry in a cool oven for 10 to 15 minutes, then process as above.

Metal Blade   *To chop whole blanched toasted almonds:* Allow to cool before processing.

Metal Blade   *To grind almonds* (useful when ground almonds are not available): Use whole blanched almonds. Put in the processor bowl, insert pusher in the feed tube and process continuously at maximum speed until finely ground.

To store: Place the nuts in a sealed container in a cool place, the refrigerator or freezer. Storage at room temperature may cause rancidity.

ANCHOVIES
Metal Blade   *To chop:* Put the anchovies in the processor bowl. To remove excessive saltiness, arrange them in a single layer barely covered with cold milk and leave to soak for 30 minutes, then pour off the excess milk. Make sure the metal blade is properly seated and

process until the anchovies are chopped or turned into a paste according to your requirements. Switch off the machine twice during processing, scraping down the sides of the bowl.

Metal Blade   *To make your own anchovy paste:* Drain the oil from a can of anchovies. Combine 75 g (3 oz) unsalted butter and the anchovies in the processor bowl and process until smooth. Store the paste in the refrigerator for up to one month.

ANGELICA

Slicing Disc (Coarse if available)   *To slice into matchsticks* (only larger quantities are suitable): Process six to eight 4 cm (1½ in) squares together. Place close together in an upright block. Attach the slicing disc and place the block carefully into the feed tube against the disc. Insert the pusher and apply only gentle pressure. Process at slow speed if your machine allows.

Metal Blade   *To chop:* Cut the angelica into strips and drop through the feed tube while the motor is running. Switch off immediately the angelica is sufficiently chopped.

To store: Place in a screw-top container to prevent drying out. If, when required, the angelica seems to be sticking together in one lump, soak in cold water for 10 minutes; drain, then dry and use as desired.

APPLES

Metal Blade   *To chop roughly:* Quarter the apples, remove the core and peel if wished. Place up to twelve apple quarters evenly in the processor bowl. Process constantly for 10 seconds, then pulse to complete the chopping.

Metal Blade   *To chop finely:* Place up to twelve apple quarters evenly in the bowl and process continuously.

Metal Blade   *To purée raw apples:* Drop the apple quarters rapidly through the feed tube while the motor is running. Process until smooth. Up to 24 apple quarters can be processed at any one time. When processing large quantities, to prevent discoloration add a few drops of lemon juice through the feed tube after every four or five apple quarters.

Metal Blade   *To purée cooked apples:* Place all the apples in the processor bowl and process until smooth.

Slicing Disc   *To slice:* Place one apple quarter into the feed tube with one flat side against the blade. Cover with a second apple quarter, placing the thin side against the thick to obtain an even layer. Arrange another layer of apple quarters on top and repeat until within 1 cm (½ in) of the top of the feed tube. Insert the pusher into position, apply gentle pressure and switch on the machine. Switch off between processing each batch. Do not remove from the bowl unless there is too great a quantity. To avoid discoloration when producing a large batch, add a few drops of lemon juice through the feed tube after every four or five apple slices.

APRICOTS

Metal Blade   *To chop dried apricots:* Place the apricots in the processor bowl and pulse until the size required is reached.

Metal Blade   *To purée cooked dried apricots:* Place the apricots all together in the processor bowl with three or four tablespoons of the cooking juices and process at maximum speed until puréed. Scrape down the sides of the bowl once during processing.

Metal Blade   *To chop fresh apricots:* Skin if desired and remove the stones (apricot stones can cause havoc in the food processor). Chop in the same way as for dried apricots.

Metal Blade   *To purée fresh apricots:* After skinning (if desired) and removing the stones, process in the same way as for dried apricots and then use in fruit fools or mixed with sugar as an apricot sauce.

Slicing Disc   *To slice fresh apricots:* Halve the fruits and remove the stones. Pile the apricots in the feed tube so that they all have the cut-side downwards, then insert the pusher into the feed tube before switching on the machine. Apply gentle pressure and switch off the machine in between assembling each batch of apricots.

To store: Fresh fruit should be used as soon as possible. It may be stored in the freezer, but some of the fresh taste will be lost.

AUBERGINES

Slicing Disc (preferably coarse)   *To slice raw aubergines:* Choose firm shiny aubergines that are as straight as possible. Top and tail and peel if wished and cut each aubergine vertically in half or, in the case of a large aubergine, into quarters. Then using the pusher as a measure, cut the aubergine into lengths that will fit vertically into the feed tube. Place one piece of aubergine into the feed tube against the disc, using gentle pressure and using subsequent pieces instead of the pusher, process one after the other. However, you must use the pusher to process the last piece. You will find that you can add the pieces one after the other without switching off the machine. Dégorge (salt to remove the bitter juices) after the aubergine is sliced, otherwise the aubergines will become too limp to achieve even slices.

Metal Blade   *To pulp cooked aubergines:* Drop the pieces of flesh through the feed tube while the motor is running.

BABY FOODS

Metal Blade   *To prepare:* The food processor enables you to prepare fresh foods for your baby. Cook a few extra vegetables or a little more white fish or chicken when preparing the family meal, then purée as much as is required for the infant. Remember to remove chicken skin and all fish bones before processing.

BACON

It is vital to remove as much rind as possible from the bacon before processing. The fat tends to cause the bacon to stick to the metal blade.

Metal Blade   *To chop raw bacon:* Switch on the machine and add the rashers two or three at a time through the feed tube. Switch off as soon as the bacon is chopped.

Metal Blade   *To chop fried bacon:* Blot the crisply fried de-rinded rashers with kitchen paper, switch on the machine and add the rashers singly while the motor is running. As soon as the last rasher has been dropped through the feed tube switch off, then pulse to achieve even-sized fragments. Use as a garnish for soups and stews. Will store in the refrigerator for 24 hours or the freezer for one month.

BANANA

Metal Blade   *To mash:* Remove the peel and break the banana into two or three pieces, placing up to three bananas in the processor bowl. Process at maximum speed, scraping down the sides of the bowl once during processing. Do not process for too long or the banana will purée. To prevent discoloration add a few drops of fresh lemon juice during the final seconds. To make a light less-fattening sauce to serve with desserts add one or two tablespoons of stiffly beaten egg white and sugar to the mashed banana and pulse two or three times only.

Slicing Disc   *To slice:* Choose bananas that are as straight as possible and these should be ripe but not soft. Peel the fruit and remove one slice from the bottom to provide a firm edge. Halve the bananas or cut into pieces that will fit the feed tube. Place two pieces of banana in an upright position side by side on the slicing disc. Insert the pusher (use gentle pressure only or the bananas will mash) and switch on the machine, preferably at low speed. Switch off the machine between processing each batch. Curvy bananas can sometimes be gently reshaped by rolling between the hands before putting into the processor.

BEANS, GREEN

Slicing Disc   *To slice runner beans:* First top, tail and remove the string from the beans using a sharp knife. Using the pusher as a guide, cut the prepared beans into lengths which will fit into the feed tube. Stack the beans together and insert vertically into the feed tube against the slicing disc. Using firm pressure on the pusher, process the beans to even slices. Switch off the machine between each batch.

Slicing Disc   *To slice rounded French beans* (not thin French beans which are unsuitable): Top, tail and remove the strings and using the base of the pusher as a guide, cut the beans into sizes that will fit horizontally into the feed tube. Place the beans into the feed tube one on top of the other against the disc, insert the pusher and use gentle pressure while processing. Switch off the motor between each batch. Frozen beans, because they are partially cooked during blanching, are unsuitable for slicing.

BEETROOT

Grating Disc (preferably coarse)   *To shred:* Cut the peeled beetroot into sections that will fit the feed tube. Place beetroot pieces into the feed tube, insert the pusher (apply gentle pressure only on cooked beetroot and firm pressure on raw beetroot) and process. There is no need to switch off the machine between batches. Do not overfill when processing cooked beetroot.

Slicing Disc   *To slice:* Cut the beetroot in half lengthwise and if there is room in the feed tube, place the two pieces head to tail, cut-sides facing each other. Insert the pusher and use gentle pressure during processing. Switch off the machine between each batch.

Slicing Disc   *To cut into matchsticks:* First trim the beetroot by hand into a block which will fit into the feed tube. Using a sharp knife and chopping board cut vertically into 6 mm (¼ in) slices. Place the stack vertically into the feed tube, thin ends against the slicing disc. Apply gentle pressure on the pusher, then switch on the machine and process into matchsticks. Switch off between processing each batch.

Metal Blade   *To purée:* Drop pieces through the feed tube while the motor is running, making sure that the top of the feed tube is covered to prevent beetroot juices spattering out. If you boil your own beetroots, you can get them to the softness that you require. In salads a beetroot that is slightly on the raw side is often preferable. Try cooking beetroots in the microwave oven.

BERRIES

Metal Blade   *To purée or pulp:* Put fresh soft berries (*raspberries, blackberries, loganberries* and *strawberries*) into the processor bowl and process continuously. To purée frozen berries put two handsful of fruit into the processor bowl, switch on the machine and add the remainder through the feed tube while the motor is running. To purée cooked berries place the fruit and juice in the processor bowl and process continuously, making sure that the pusher is inserted in the feed tube.

To purée fresh *gooseberries* and *blackcurrants* drop these through the feed tube while the motor is running, keeping the top of the feed tube covered to prevent spattering. To process cooked blackcurrants and gooseberries, place in the processor bowl with their liquid and process continuously. Soft fruits containing seeds or pips should be passed through a sieve after processing as the food processor does not eliminate these. Use pulped or puréed fruit for fools, ice cream, baby foods, milk shakes and sauces.

Slicing Disc   *To slice fresh gooseberries:* Fill the feed tube with the prepared fruit, insert the pusher and use medium pressure while processing. Switch off between processing each batch. Although slices will be of even thickness they will not necessarily be of uniform shape. Large dessert gooseberries can sometimes be placed upright and side by side in the feed tube. Remove a thin slice from both ends and stack. Frozen gooseberries can be sliced in a similar way to fresh gooseberries provided the manufacturers of the food processor permit this.

Coarse Slicing Disc   *To slice fresh strawberries:* Only fresh firm berries are suitable. It is essential to choose really firm fruit and apply only gentle pressure on the pusher. Remember to top and tail strawberries before processing as any stray stalks will be difficult to extract. To achieve perfect slices for garnish select large berries and remove a thin slice from the pointed end, then stack as for gooseberries.

BISCUITS

Metal Blade   *To grind coarsely:* Put the biscuits into the bowl, insert the pusher in the feed tube and pulse to the desired texture.

Metal Blade   *To grind finely or pulverize:* Switch on the machine and add the biscuits through the feed tube and process until powdered. Cover the top of the feed tube while processing to prevent biscuits from spattering. Ground biscuits will keep well in a covered container in the larder, refrigerator or freezer. Sweet and dry biscuits can be processed in a similar way.

Grate sweet biscuits to use as bases for cheesecakes or similar flans. They are also useful as toppings on fruit desserts; one of my favourite recipes is Banana Mush in which I purée bananas with sugar, then top with grated sweet biscuits and thickened cream. Use ground dry biscuits for bases for savoury flans or mix with grated cheese for savoury toppings.

BLACKBERRIES
See Berries

BLACKCURRANTS
See Berries

BREADCRUMBS
Metal Blade   *To make fresh soft breadcrumbs:* Switch on the machine, tear the bread into pieces and drop them through the feed tube one after the other. Place the pusher in the feed tube to prevent the breadcrumbs from spattering but make sure that you do not overload the machine. An uncut loaf is easiest to prepare for breadcrumb-making because the crusts can be removed quickly. Break the bread into chunks before processing. Sliced bread can be used without removing the crusts because they are so soft.

Metal Blade   *To make dried breadcrumbs or raspings:* Bake or toast the crusts or slices of the bread until they are dry. Break up and treat as for fresh breadcrumbs.

To store: Fresh breadcrumbs can be stored in a covered container in the freezer. They only have a short life in the refrigerator. Dried breadcrumbs store well in an airtight container in a cool place, refrigerator or the freezer.

Fresh breadcrumbs are suitable for use in puddings or for coatings. Dried breadcrumbs (raspings) are suitable for use in fish or meat balls or as coatings for frying. To make buttered crumbs pour melted butter through the feed tube after the bread is crumbed and mix briefly.

BRUSSELS SPROUTS

Slicing Disc (fine)   *To slice raw:* Top and tail and wash in the usual way, then fill the feed tube with the Brussels sprouts. Insert the pusher using firm pressure and process until shredded. Switch off between processing each batch. If you have never thought of using Brussels sprouts in salads give them a try using the food processor. Add salad dressing or mayonnaise to make a perfect coleslaw.

Metal Blade   *To chop cooked:* Place the drained sprouts in the processor bowl and pulse until coarsely chopped. Serve as a vegetable base for soup or sauce. Cooked Brussels sprouts and cooked chestnuts can be chopped together to produce a Christmassy vegetable.

BURGERS

Metal Blade   *To make burgers:* Cut the raw meat into 2.5 cm (1 in) cubes leaving some fat on if you prefer a moister softer burger. Place not more than 225 g (8 oz) prepared meat in the processor bowl and pulse until the meat is sufficiently chopped. Switch off, remove the meat from the processor bowl and then repeat with another batch. If you are chopping onions or other ingredients at the same time it is better to do these first. They can then be left in the bowl when the meat (or the first batch of the meat) is added. For moist light burgers the meat should not be over-chopped. For open-textured burgers prepare the ingredients separately, then mix by hand in a large bowl. Use a light touch when shaping the burgers and if using a burger press do not push the meat down too firmly or all the air will be completely pressed out, giving dense and tough results.

BUTTER

Metal Blade   *To soften butter for creaming or spreading:* Cut refrigerator-hard butter into 2.5 cm (1 in) cubes. Arrange in a single layer in the bowl and pulse until the butter begins to soften, then switch on at maximum speed and process to the required consistency.

Slicing Disc   *To slice:* Cut a 250 g (½ lb) refrigerator-hard butter in half lengthwise, then chill in the freezer for 30 minutes. Insert one piece of butter into the feed tube, insert the pusher and process using only gentle pressure. Switch off the machine before inserting the second piece of butter.

Use butter slices for spreading and in particular when you wish to use measured amounts for, e.g., slimming or low-cholesterol diets. The butter slices will soon soften at room temperature, so should be returned to the refrigerator immediately after processing.

Coarse Grating Disc or Julienne Disc   *To grate or shred:* First cut into blocks which will fit the feed tube, then freeze the pieces until hard, taking care they do not stick together during chilling. Refrigerator-hard butter does not shred well. Put a butter block in the feed tube, insert the pusher and, applying gentle pressure, switch on the machine and process as many butter sticks as you require. Switch of between batches and if a large quantity is being shredded remove from the freezer a few at a time. Use shredded butter for topping vegetables, for service at table or in a cake, pudding or sauce recipes where quick even softening or melting is required.

Metal Blade   *To make savoury butter* (Maître d'Hôtel butter): Cut the butter into cubes, place in the processor bowl and process until soft, adding chopped herbs to taste. Form into cylinders and roll up in greaseproof paper, then freeze and slice as required with a sharp knife.

Metal Blade   *To make savoury shredded butter:* Cut the butter into cubes, then process at maximum speed until soft, adding chopped herbs or spices. Form the softened mixture into a shape that will fit into the feed tube, then freeze until required.

Coarse Grating Disc or Julienne Disc   *To shred:* Process as for shredded butter.

Metal Blade   *To make butter icing:* Put butter cubes and sugar together in the bowl before switching on the machine. Place the pusher in the feed tube to prevent the sugar (particularly icing sugar) from coming out in clouds and scrape down the sides of the bowl twice during processing.

Metal Blade   *To make butter icing topping:* Make in the same way as butter icing using only sufficient sugar to lightly sweeten, and add a few drops of food colouring and flavouring (such as orange flower water, or rose water or almond essence) to the mixture. Freeze in pieces that fit the feed tube, then shred as for savoury butters. Shredded butter must be frozen immediately after processing; whilst still hard, place in containers which are big enough to prevent the butter from packing down. These butters are particularly attractive when sprinkled over individual fruit tartlets.

CABBAGE

Slicing Disc   *To shred coarsely:* To shred cabbage coarsely for salads cut into chunks that will fit into the feed tube and insert, cut sides down. Use firm pressure on the pusher and switch off between each addition.

Grating Disc   *To shred finely:* Attach the grater, coarse or fine, and add chunks of cabbage one after the other through the feed tube while the machine is running. Press each piece down well with the pusher, keeping the top of the feed tube covered during processing.

Metal Blade   *To chop cooked cabbage:* Place two portions at a time in the processor bowl and pulse to the desired texture. Remove the chopped cabbage before processing the next batch.

CAKES

Preparation varies depending upon the recipe and ingredients being used.

Metal Blade   *Basic all-in-one mixtures:* Put all the ingredients into the processor bowl at the same time and process only until all the ingredients are incorporated. Switch on for about 10 seconds, then scrape down the sides of the bowl and process for a further 5 to 15 seconds. Further beating is undesirable.

Metal Blade   *Creamed mixtures* (recipes in which the butter and sugar are beaten together before other ingredients are added): Cube the butter and place in the processor bowl with the sugar, then switch on and add the eggs one at a time through the feed tube, together with one or two tablespoons of flour to prevent the mixture from curdling. Add the remaining flour in two parts at the end of the mixing time. To do this, remove the lid, add half the flour, then pulse once or twice until the flour particles disappear. Repeat with the remaining flour. Do not insert the pusher while making creamed mixture cakes as these require all the additional air that they can get.

Although you can make double and treble quantities if you have a large-capacity processor, curdling is more likely to take place. The reason for this is that the creamed butter and sugar become warm and the cold egg, on blending, causes some of the fat particles to solidify on contact.

To lessen the chances of curdling you may find this method of mixing better. Put the eggs and sugar together in the processor bowl and process until thick. Scrape down the sides of the bowl, switch on the machine and add the cubed butter through the feed tube while the motor is still running. Add the remaining ingredients except the flour and process until well mixed. Remove the processor lid and add the flour in two separate batches, pulsing each time until all the particles are incorporated.

Metal Blade   *Rubbed-in mixtures:* Place the flour in the bowl with the cubed butter and insert the pusher into the feed tube. Process until the mixture resembles crumbs. If the butter is hard you may find it better to pulse rather than process continuously. Add the remaining ingredients and process until just mixed to an even texture. When making several cakes prepare the butter and flour mixture in batches in the food processor, then replace each batch and add the remaining ingredients.

CANDIED AND GLACÉ FRUIT

Metal Blade   *To chop glacé cherries:* Rinse away the syrup in cold water and dry the fruit lightly. Place the cherries in the processor bowl and pulse until chopped. Glacé cherries become finely chopped very quickly and if over-processed adhere to the metal blade.

Slicing Disc   *To slice candied orange and lemon peel:* Pile several pieces of peel on top of one another and then place in the feed tube cut sides down. Insert the pusher and apply gentle pressure when processing. Switch off between each batch.

Metal Blade   *To chop candied orange and lemon peel:* Switch on the machine and add the slices through the feed tube while the motor is still running, switching off immediately all the slices have been added. Continue pulsing to the required size.

To use chopped fruit in cakes or puddings process the unrinsed fruit with part of the flour from the recipe. Remove the fruit from the processor bowl, then continue with your cake recipe, replacing the chopped fruit at the end.

CAPERS
Metal Blade   *To chop:* Switch on the machine and drop the capers through the feed tube while the motor is running.

CARROTS
Metal Blade   *To chop raw:* For use in soups or casseroles, cut the prepared carrots into chunks. Place in the processor bowl and process continuously until the carrots are chopped. The pieces will be of uneven size but in this case it is not important.

Slicing Disc   *To slice raw:* Attach the slicing disc and arrange the prepared carrots thick end downwards against the blade, filling the tube with as many carrots as it will take. The carrots or carrot pieces should not be taller than the length of the tube. Insert the pusher and process each batch of carrots separately.

Slicing Disc   *To slice lengthways:* Cut the pieces to fit widthways into the feed tube. The carrot placed at the bottom should have a sliver removed so that this piece fits firmly against the slicing disc. Insert the pusher and use medium pressure. Slice each batch separately.

Coarse Grating Disc or Julienne Disc   *To shred:* Longer strips will be obtained if the carrots are positioned horizontally as above.

Grating Disc   *To grate finely:* Put the prepared carrots in the feed tube. There is no need for especial care.

Insert the pusher and use medium pressure while processing.

Chipper Disc For larger pieces place the carrots horizontally in the feed tube, then insert the pusher and use light pressure while processing. Switch off between processing each batch.

Metal Blade   *To purée cooked carrots:* Insert through the feed tube while the machine is running. Scrape down the sides of the bowl twice during processing.

CAULIFLOWER

Metal Blade   *To chop raw:* For salads break the florettes from the stems and put in the processor bowl. Pulse to the required size.

Metal Blade   *To purée cooked cauliflower:* Feed through the tube while the machine is running. Scrape down the sides of the bowl twice during processing.

To make a quick cauliflower soup purée the cooked cauliflower with a thin Béchamel sauce and flavour with grated cheese.

CELERIAC

Coarse Grating Disc   *To grate:* Celeriac is very hard and dense and it is difficult to cut through. Use a sharp knife and a wooden chopping board. First peel the celeriac and squeeze a little lemon juice over the outside to prevent it from discolouring. As quickly as possible cut the vegetable into chunks. Provided the shapes will fit into the feed tube it does not matter whether these are slivers or cubes. Quickly place the pieces in the feed tube against the grating disc. Insert the pusher and use firm pressure while processing. Sprinkle the celeriac in the food processor bowl with lemon juice before processing the next batch, then mix with salad dressing at once.

CELERY

Metal Blade *To chop for casseroles or stews:* Break
washed and trimmed celery stalks into even lengths,
place in the processor bowl and pulse until sufficiently
chopped.

Slicing Disc *To slice:* Cut the celery stalks into lengths
that will fit vertically into the feed tube, leaving a 1 cm
(½ in) head space. Insert the pusher and while using
gentle pressure switch on the machine. Switch off
between processing each batch. If celery slices are to be
used immediately use the thin slicing disc, but for more
regular and crisper results use a coarser disc. Sometimes
slivers of celery become stuck in the slicing blade,
causing it to become unseated. Remove these carefully
with a fork. This is due to faulty stacking of the feed
tube which must be pre-loaded with celery before
switching on the machine.

CHEESE

Grating Disc *To grate:* Cut the cheese into chunks or
cubes. It does not matter if these are misshapen. Insert
the pusher and apply medium to heavy pressure, switch
on the machine and process continuously. Do not
overfill the bowl or the cheese will become packed
down and stick together in lumps. Stale dry cheese
grates more successfully than fresh. Fresh cheese tends
to stick to the disc, so place the cheese in the freezer for
10 to 15 minutes before processing. Cheese may be
shredded directly from the frozen state, but after thawing, cheese may be too crumbly. Make sure that the
grating or slicing discs are completely dry before at-
taching and dust lightly with flour before starting.
Freeze grated cheese in a large airy container, shaking it
from time to time during freezing.

Slicing Disc *To slice:* Firm cheeses such as Emmenthal
and Gruyère slice well. Cut into pieces that will fit the

feed tube, making sure that the bottoms of all pieces are smoothly cut. Insert the pusher and using light pressure switch on and process. Switch off between each batch.

Metal Blade   *To blend cottage and curd cheeses* (for dips or cheesecakes): Put the cheese in the processor bowl and process until smooth. Scrape down the sides of the bowl twice during processing. Chopped herbs may be processed at the same time.

Metal Blade   *To chop hard cheese:* For sandwich fillings, spreads or potted cheeses. Break into pieces and add through the feed tube while the motor is running. Butter can be added at the same time.

CHESTNUTS

See Nuts. Also see note at end of Brussels Sprouts section.

CHICKEN

See Poultry

CHICKEN LIVERS

Metal Blade   *To chop:* Remove any membranes and wash the livers in cold water and pat dry before processing. Put the prepared chicken livers in the bowl and pulse once or twice only to chop. Chicken livers are frequently used in pâtés; after cooking they can be processed with softened butter and spices to produce the simplest and tastiest pâté.

CHICORY

Slicing Disc   *To slice:* Process two to three trimmed chicory pieces together at one time, packing them tightly in the feed tube. You may find it easiest to place the two outside pieces thick-side down and the third one in the middle with the pointed end downwards. Insert the pusher and apply firm pressure before switching on the machine.

CHOCOLATE

Dessert chocolate should be refrigerated for at least 30 minutes before processing. Block cooking chocolate benefits from short spells in the freezer.

Grating Disc   *To grate bars:* Insert three or four half-bars of dessert chocolate, whether milk or plain, with the narrow edges against the grating disc. Apply gentle pressure on the pusher to obtain thicker shreds and firm pressure to obtain finer shreds.

Grating Disc   *To grate block cooking chocolate:* Break off lumps from the block and place in the feed tube to reach at least half-way up. Insert the pusher and process in the same way as for dessert chocolate. Small pieces of chocolate do not grate successfully as they are inclined to slide between the lid and the disc. It is better to chop these and use in recipes requiring chocolate. Both grated and chopped chocolate melt quickly and can usually be stirred straight into hot liquids such as milky drinks.

Metal Blade   *To chop chocolate:* Place misshapened and small fragments of chocolate into the bowl. Insert the pusher in the feed tube to prevent the chocolate from spattering, then switch on the machine until the chocolate is processed into small fragments.

To store: Finely grated chocolate keeps well in the freezer or refrigerator and may be used as toppings for desserts or to decorate cakes.

CITRUS FRUITS

Juicing Attachment   *To juice:* A special juicing attachment is preferable. Follow the instructions supplied.

Metal Blade   *To juice:* Without the special attachment the metal blade can be used, but the juice must be strained before serving. Peel the fruit, then halve crosswise and remove the pips. Do not worry if a few pips find their way into the bowl as they will be removed later. Cut the fruit into smallish chunks and place in the processor bowl. Switch on the machine at maximum power and process until the fruit is puréed. Strain the pulp mixture through a fine sieve into a bowl or jug, pressing the pulp down firmly with a wooden spoon. The pulp can be thrown away. This method is suitable for four lemons or oranges or two grapefruit. Larger quantities producing more pulp are difficult to cope with.

Metal Blade *To grate rind:* Pare away the outside layer of the fruit, making sure that no white pith is attached. Dry the pieces between sheets of kitchen paper. Switch on the machine and feed through the tube while the motor is running. Scrape down the sides of the bowl once, as soon as all the pieces have been inserted, then process until finely chopped.

   To store: Spread out the chopped rind in a smooth thin layer on a freezer tray, freeze until hard, then pack loosely in a small container and keep in the freezer.

Slicing Disc *To slice citrus peel for use in marmalade or for making chocolate-covered confectionery:* Using a sharp knife make a deep cut through the peel from top to bottom at four equal intervals. Peel away the quarters by hand. Pare away part of the white pith and pile the skins on top of one another. Press a stack of peel into the tube, pressing the thin edges against the blade. Apply gentle pressure with the pusher and switch on the machine. Switch off the machine between processing each batch.

Slicing Disc *To make lemon slices:* Wash and dry the lemons and remove a slice from the top and bottom. Cut in half lengthways and remove any obvious pips with a pointed knife. Place the lemon halves, either together or separately, vertically in the feed tube against the slicing disc. Nestle the lemon against the side of the tube furthest away from the direction of the cutting edge, which should first slice into the peel. (The slices will be jagged and uneven if the slicing disc first cuts through the soft flesh.) Apply medium pressure on the pusher and switch on the machine. Switch off between processing each batch. Using a fork, carefully remove any sliced pips that may have lodged in the slicing disc between processing each batch. For decorative lemon slices pare away four to six thin slivers of peel lengthwise at intervals round the lemon before halving. Firm oranges and limes may be treated in the same way as lemons.

COCONUT

Before processing pare away the brown outer skin from the coconut pieces and leave the coconut uncovered for 6 hours to give it a chance to dry out.

Grating Disc   *To grate:* Fill the feed tube with chunks of peeled coconut and use medium pressure on the pusher while processing.

Metal Blade   *To chop:* Cut the peeled coconut into approximately 2.5 cm (1 in) pieces; switch on the machine and while the motor is running, add the pieces through the feed tube.

Metal Blade   *To colour chopped coconut:* Add a few drops of food colouring to the chopped coconut and process until mixed to an even colour.

Metal Blade   *To sweeten coconut for use in toppings:* Add 2 or 3 tablespoons of granulated sugar to the chopped coconut and process until well mixed.

To store: Store the coconut in a covered container in the freezer. If a brown effect is required, first spread the coconut in the grill pan and brown carefully, stirring the coconut from time to time, then store in an airtight container in the larder.

COFFEE (not suitable for all machines)

Metal Blade   *To grind:* Place the roasted beans in the processor bowl and switch on for 3 seconds. Switch off briefly and repeat until the coffee is of the required texture. Make sure that the pusher is in the feed tube during processing. It is preferable to use freshly ground coffee at once, but it may be stored for a short time in an airtight container.

CORNFLAKES

Metal Blade   *To pulverize:* Place the cornflakes, 3 or 4 heaped tablespoons at a time, in the processor bowl and process continuously. Make sure that the pusher is in the feed tube during processing. Use as a coating when frying fish or escalopes of veal or chicken.

Metal Blade   *To crush:* Place the cornflakes in the processor bowl and pulse for the required texture. To make a savoury flan base pour in a few tablespoons of melted butter and mix briefly, then press the mixture into a cake or flan tin. For sweet flan bases such as cheesecake add a few tablespoons of sugar during processing.

COURGETTES

Slicing Disc   *To slice:* Choose firm courgettes and bear in mind the size of the feed tube when purchasing. Wash, dry, top and tail the courgettes. Cut into pieces that will fit upright in the feed tube against the slicing disc. Use firm pressure on the courgettes with the pusher and switch on the machine. Switch off the motor between processing each batch.

Thick Slicing Disc   *To make matchsticks:* Cut the trimmed courgettes into pieces that will fit horizontally into the feed tube. Place as many pieces into the feed tube against the blade as possible, insert the pusher and use light pressure while processing. Switch off between each batch. Remove the courgette slices from the processor bowl and, stacking three or four slices on top of one another on a wooden board, cut thinly into matchsticks with a sharp knife. It is easier to do this by hand than to try and use the processor.

Grating Disc   *To shred:* Cut the courgettes into 2.5 cm (1 in) lengths, place in the feed tube and use firm pressure on the pusher while processing. To make zucchini, dropped scones or pancakes, sprinkle the grated courgettes with salt and leave for 30 minutes, then strain through a sieve and press out as much moisture as possible. Stir into a pancake batter and shallow fry a tablespoon at a time on both sides until the pancakes are golden.

CRABMEAT

Metal Blade   *To chop:* Put the crabmeat into the processor bowl and pulse until chopped. Use in salads or mousses.

CREAM

Metal Blade or Whisking Attachment   *To whip:* Cream cannot be whipped to a large volume in the food processor but will thicken very successfully, whether you use the metal blade or the whisking attachment. Do not attempt to process less than 150 ml (¼ pt) or more than 300 ml (½ pt) at one time in the standard-sized processor bowl. For most successful results place the cream, bowl and blade in the refrigerator for 30 minutes before processing. Switch on the machine and pour double or whipping cream in a thin stream through the feed tube while the motor is running. Put the pusher in position and process only until the cream thickens. (Over-beating will cause clotting and separation; should this happen, strain away the milky liquid and add a spot of salt and you will have produced some wonderful dairy butter.) Use the thickened cream for cake fillings or in any recipe where thick cream is used as a component part, but not as a piped decorative topping. For sweetened cream add a little icing sugar to the cream during processing. Thickened cream can be frozen if desired but tends to thin out when thawed. Shredded chocolate and thickened cream mixed together are a delicious topping for fruit salad.

CRYSTALLIZED FRUIT
See Candied and Glacé Fruit

CUCUMBER
Slicing Disc   *To slice:* Try to choose straight cucumbers with diameters narrow enough to fit into the feed tube. If the cucumbers are too wide, pare away a thick layer of skin, then chop this separately and use in soups. Remove a slice from the thick end of the cucumber and cut into lengths that will fit into the feed tube, leaving a 1 cm (½ in) head space. Place one or two pieces upright in the feed tube against the disc. If the pieces are too big to insert two lengths side by side, insert only one, placing it against the right-hand side of the feed tube if the blade revolves to the right, so that the blade is constantly pushing the cucumber towards this side. Making sure that the top end of the cucumber is level, insert the pusher in the feed tube. Apply gentle but firm pressure, switch on the machine and switch off between each batch. For decorative slices use unpeeled cucumber; vertically pare slivers of the skin away with a potato peeler or canelle knife before processing.

Metal Blade   *To purée (for use in soups):* Cut the cucumber into 2.5 cm (1 in) chunks. Switch on the machine and drop the chunks one by one into the feed tube while the motor is running and process to a purée. The particles will not be as fine as when liquidized, but most people find the results highly satisfactory.

CUCUMBERS, PICKLED

Metal Blade   *To chop:* Cut into 2.5 cm (1 in) chunks, place in the food processor bowl and pulse to the required size.

Slicing Disc   *To slice:* Cut in half crossways and place the two pieces side by side in the feed tube against the slicing disc. Insert the pusher and use gentle pressure while processing.

CUSTARD

Metal Blade   *To make custard from powder:* Put 300 ml (½ pt) cold milk into the processor bowl, switch on the machine and pour the custard powder and sugar through the feed tube. Pour into a saucepan, add the remaining milk, then bring to the boil and cook, stirring continuously, for 2 or 3 minutes until the custard is thickened.

Metal Blade   *To make egg custards:* Put the eggs and sugar and flavouring into the processor bowl and process until light and fluffy. While the motor is running add warm milk through the feed tube. Strain into a saucepan and continue cooking according to the recipe.

Metal Blade   *To remove lumps:* Switch on the motor and pour the cooked custard through the feed tube, then immediately insert the pusher to prevent spattering and process until the custard becomes smooth.

DRIED FRUIT

Metal Blade   *To chop:* Place in the processor bowl and pulse to the desired texture. Sticky fruits, such as dates and glacé cherries, are best when processed with part of the flour from the recipe. Currants, stoned raisins and sultanas require very little processing to chop. When using in cake and pudding recipes add them just before the flour.

DUCK
See Poultry

EGGS

Metal Blade   *To beat lightly:* Switch on the motor and add the eggs through the feed tube. As soon as all the eggs have been added the mixture should have been beaten sufficiently. Do not use the processor for beating just one egg unless other liquid ingredients are being included. A minimum of four egg yolks can be beaten together at the same time.

Metal Blade or Whisking Attachment   *To beat egg whites:* Use the metal blade for foaming; use the whisking attachment for beating to soft peaks. Follow the manufacturer's directions for the recommended quantity of egg whites. To achieve stiff peaks and greatest volume egg whites must be beaten traditionally in a grease-free bowl using a balloon rotary or electric beater. Use the whisking attachment to beat eggs and sugar mixtures to a mousse-like consistency for whisked sponges etc. This cannot be achieved using the metal blade.

Metal Blade   *To chop hard-boiled eggs:* Halve the shelled eggs and place in the processor bowl and pulse to the required texture.

Metal Blade   *To chop or sieve hard-boiled egg yolks:* The egg yolks must be completely cold before processing. Pulse extra quickly but only briefly. Over-processing will result in a paste. For sandwich fillings process halved eggs with mayonnaise to taste or include the butter that you would normally use for spreading and process to a paste. Scrape down the sides of the bowl once or twice during processing. When chopping hard-boiled eggs it is desirable to put the pusher into the feed tube to prevent spattering.

FENNEL

Slicing Disc   *To chop:* Remove the stalks, cut a slice from the base of the fennel, then cut in half or quarters lengthways. Place one or two pieces at a time vertically in the feed tube, stalk side up, insert the pusher and using medium pressure, process each batch separately. Use in salads or as a cooked vegetable.

FISH

Metal Blade   *To chop raw fish:* Cut into pieces and place in the processor bowl before switching on or drop continuously through the feed tube while the motor is running. Raw fish may be chopped as coarsely or finely as you wish.

Metal Blade   *To chop frozen fish steaks:* Drop one at a time through the feed tube while the motor is running. It is difficult to skin frozen fish so although unskinned frozen fish can be processed, the dark flecks will be obvious in the finished dish.

Metal Blade   *To make quennelles, fish paté or fish balls:* First process the other ingredients such as onion and carrot, adding the raw fish last.

Metal Blade   *To process cooked fish:* Make sure that all bones have been removed before processing or you will find tiny pieces of bone in the finished dish. Place in the processor bowl and pulse to flake. Continuously process for fish pastes. Left-over 'fish in sauce' dishes can be processed continuously to produce yet another fish sauce to go with vegetables and pasta. All canned fish is suitable for making mousses and patés in the food processor.

Fish cakes, whether raw or cooked, can be stored in the freezer for up to one month but you should not use frozen fish to prepare uncooked fish cakes if they are then to be frozen.

FLOUR

Metal Blade   *To sift:* Place together with other dry ingredients such as salt, baking powder or spices in the processor bowl and process for a few seconds. Sugar may then be added and the fat rubbed in without removing the flour from the bowl. If your recipe calls for sifted flour to be added after the other ingredients, the flour may be temporarily removed from the bowl and the other ingredients, such as butter and sugar for creaming, can be processed without the need to wash the bowl.

FRUIT

See individual references, Berries, Citrus Fruits etc.

GAMMON

Metal Blade   *To chop:* After removing the rind and fat, cut the gammon into cubes, place in the processor bowl and pulse to the required consistency.

Slicing Disc   *To make gammon medallions:* Cut the trimmed joint into pieces that will just fit the feed tube. Then wrap up each piece and chill in the freezer until solid, but not so frozen that each piece cannot be cut through with a sharp knife. Put the gammon pieces in the feed tube, insert the pusher and apply medium pressure while processing. Switch off the machine between batches.

GARLIC

Metal Blade   *To chop:* Garlic is usually chopped when other savoury ingredients are being mixed. Drop the garlic clove through the feed tube while the motor is running after other ingredients, such as the first piece of onion, have been processed. To help remove garlic odour from the processor bowl, process a piece of lemon rind with one or two tablespoons of boiling water, then wash and rinse the bowl in the usual way.

GHERKINS

Metal Blade   *To chop:* Place in the processor bowl and pulse to the required texture.

GINGER ROOT

Metal Blade   *To chop:* Cut the peeled ginger into 2.5 cm (1 in) chunks. Switch on the machine and add the ginger pieces through the feed tube while the motor is running. *To store:* Spread out the chopped ginger root on a tray or plate and freeze. When frozen pack lightly into small freezer containers. I use the smallest size of Tupperware pots or the square boxes obtainable from Lakeland Plastics.

GOOSEBERRIES

See Berries

GRAPEFRUIT

See Citrus Fruits

HAM

Metal Blade   *To chop large pieces:* Cut the ham into chunks, spread out in the processor bowl and pulse until suitably-sized pieces are obtained.

Metal Blade   *To chop slices:* Switch on the machine, drop the first two slices as quickly as possible through the feed tube, then switch off. Remove from the bowl and repeat with any remaining ham slices.

Slicing Disc   To obtain thin small slices cut ham joints into sizes that will just fit into the feed tube and chill in the freezer until almost frozen. Place one piece at a time in the feed tube against the slicing disc, insert the pusher and use medium pressure when processing. Switch off between batches.

Slicing Disc   To obtain thin strips roll three or four thin slices together to form a Swiss roll shape which will fit vertically into the feed tube. Wrap in a piece of greaseproof paper or clingfilm to maintain the shape and chill in the freezer until firm. When the ham roll is almost hard insert into the feed tube against the slicing disc, insert the pusher and use gentle pressure while processing.

Metal Blade   *To cream:* Drop through the feed tube while the motor is running and process until smooth.

HERBS

Metal Blade   *To chop small quantities:* Drop the herbs through the feed tube while the motor is running.

Metal Blade   *To chop larger quantities (more than a handful):* Place the herbs in the processor bowl, switch on and process continuously to the required size. Fresh herbs should be washed and patted dry with kitchen paper or a teacloth before processing. Discard all stalks. Tarragon, sage and basil leaves become very moist after chopping. Fresh rosemary leaves are difficult to chop but are manageable if frozen first. For parsley, remove the stalks and process a handful at a time.

To store: Spread the chopped herbs out on a suitable tray and fast freeze until stiff. Separate with the fingers and store in a small container in the freezer. If you prefer, add a few tablespoons of cold water to the chopped herbs in the processor bowl and process quickly to mix. Pour into ice cube trays and freeze. This is a suitable method when herbs are required for soups, stews and sauces.

Store dried herbs in airtight containers. Dry garden-fresh herbs on the stalks, then remove the stalks before chopping. Most herbs dry very satisfactorily in the microwave oven, but the stalks should be removed before drying as they can cause sparking and burning. Place the de-stalked leaves on kitchen paper, cover lightly, place in the microwave and stir with the fingers every ten seconds until the herbs are dry. Parsley needs no further processing after drying but leafy herbs should be placed in the processor bowl and processed continuously before being stored.

HORSERADISH

Metal Blade   *To chop:* Cut the peeled horseradish into 2.5 cm (1 in) chunks. Switch on the machine and drop the horseradish through the feed tube while the motor is running.

To store: Store in small containers in the refrigerator for up to two weeks. For freezer storage, first open-freeze before packing into boxes and storing for up to six months.

ICE

Metal Blade   *To crush ice cubes:* Follow the manufacturer's instructions. Switch on the machine and drop the cubes through the feed tube one at a time while the motor is running. The first two to three ice cubes should be added separately, but as soon as these are chopped the remainder can be added quite rapidly. Process no more than one tray of cubes at a time – during processing the temperature rises, causing the ice to melt. Sometimes the machine tends to move around the work surface during processing, so that it may need a steadying hand. Do not have your face directly above the open feed tube, as the ice particles may spatter in the initial stages of processing.

Parmesan Grater   *To crush with a fine or Parmesan grater:* Fill the feed tube with the ice and apply firm pressure on the pusher. Process in as many batches as you wish, transferring each to the freezer until all are crushed.

ICE CREAM

Metal Blade   *To make ice cream:* Mix the ingredients for the custard in the processor bowl before cooking. Purée raw fruit in the processor bowl (see page 34) to mix in with the custard and cream. For an extra smooth ice cream spoon into the processor when the mixture is half frozen and process quickly before completing freezing. To make a quick cold sauce switch on the motor and place small blocks of ready-made ice cream in the feed tube while the motor is running and process until liquid. Serve with desserts. Do not freeze these ice cream sauces.

KIWI FRUIT

Slicing Disc   *To slice:* Remove a thin slice from one end of the peeled kiwi fruit and place upright in the feed tube against the slicing disc. Insert the pusher and use only to hold the fruit in position. Do not press down while processing. Switch off between processing each kiwi fruit. Place the fruit two or three at a time in the processor bowl and pulse to the desired consistency. Pulped kiwi fruit provides a fresh tasting topping for rich dessert tarts or mousses.

LEMONS

See Citrus Fruits

LENTILS, SPLIT PEAS AND DRIED BEANS

Metal Blade   *To mash:* Place the cooked pulses in the processor bowl about two cupsful at a time and process continuously to the desired texture, scraping down the sides of the bowl once during processing. When making lentil or split pea soups transfer the cooked pulses to the processor bowl with a slotted spoon. After processing, return the purée to the saucepan containing the cooking liquid. Stir thoroughly and reheat. This method is quicker than processing both the liquid and solids together, because of the limited volume of the processor bowl.

LIVER

Slicing Disc   *To slice:* Before slicing liver remove cores and any membranes, rinse and dry with kitchen paper. Cut trimmed liver into portions that will fit into the feed tube, then freeze until firm but not completely frozen. Place the liver chunks one at a time into the feed tube, placing each against the slicing disc. Insert the pusher and use gentle pressure while processing. Switch off between processing each piece of liver.

Metal Blade   *To chop:* Place the raw or cooked liver, cut into chunks or slices, in the processor bowl and pulse to the required texture. Rinse the food processor bowl and blade in cold water before washing up.

MARGARINE

Hard margarine: Treat as for butter.

Soft margarine: Use wherever softened butter is recommended. Soft margarine is extremely good in pastry and blends easily in sauce making.

MARROW (Vegetable)

Metal Blade   *To purée (for use in chutneys and jams):* Cut raw peeled and seeded marrow into 2.5 cm (1 in) thick slices. Halve the slices and put into the processor bowl, the amount should reach no more than half-way up the sides. Pulse until the marrow pulps down, then process continuously to the required consistency.

A soup can be quickly made by combining cooked marrow with a white sauce.

Metal Blade   *To pulp cooked marrow:* Drain thoroughly, then put the marrow in the processor bowl and process continuously.

MEAT

Metal Blade   *To chop (for all recipes calling for mince):* The secret is not to over-chop. Over-chopping causes the finished product to be dense and somewhat tough. When preparing meat for burgers it is desirable to leave a little of the fat on the meat when trimming and then the burgers will be moister and more tasty (see also page 37). For even chopping, place up to 225 g (½ lb) cubed meat in the processor bowl in a single layer and pulse to the required texture.

Slicing Disc   *To slice raw meat (for stir-fry dishes or medallions):* Cut the trimmed meat into chunks that will fit into the feed tube, then in the case of fresh meat freeze until solid but not completely frozen. Insert one piece into the feed tube close to the slicing disc, insert the pusher and apply medium pressure while processing. Switch off between batches.

Slicing Disc   *To slice cooked meat:* Refrigerate until cold. (Do not slice roast meat while still warm.) Cut into lumps and stack the pieces in the feed tube so that they will be cut across the grain and proceed as for raw meat.

MAYONNAISE

To make mayonnaise in the food processor use recipes that are specially designed for the processor. The ingredients must be all at the same temperature – this can be difficult as the temperature rises while the machine is in operation. Either use whole eggs or make sure the oil is warm. To heat pour the oil into a jug and place the jug in a pan of very hot water. Stir the oil occasionally until it is uniformly warm. In the initial stages of beating eggs for mayonnaise it sometimes helps to raise one side of the food processor approximately 2.5 cm (1 in) while processing, but this should only be done if the manufacturer of your machine permits it. To enrich mayonnaise add cream after the mayonnaise has thickened and process briefly to mix in. To make herb mayonnaise add the herbs after the eggs.

MUSHROOMS

Metal Blade   *To chop:* Place the mushrooms with or without stalks in a single or double layer in the processor bowl and pulse to the required size. To chop for flavouring use either whole mushrooms or stalks alone, cutting if necessary into sizes that can be dropped through the feed tube while the motor is running. Process continuously to a coarse paste, scraping down the sides of the bowl once during processing.

Slicing Disc   *To slice:* For mushrooms for less important dishes, fill the feeder tube with mushrooms, insert the pusher and apply light pressure while processing. Switch off the machine between each batch. For dishes of medium importance use button mushrooms and cut the stalks level with the caps; fill the feed tube with the mushrooms, placing them open-sides down. Insert the pusher and apply gentle pressure while processing. Switch off between each batch.

Fine Slicing Disc   For garnish or special dishes place the trimmed button mushrooms on their sides with the caps against the flatter sides of the feed tube. Pack carefully in rows of three or four, layering until the feed tube is nearly filled. Insert the pusher and apply gentle pressure while processing. Switch off between processing each batch. Do not process more than the bowl can take or the fine slices will be crushed.

Only field mushrooms need careful cleaning and peeling.

Cultivated mushrooms are mostly grown in special conditions and require only wiping before use.

NUTS

Metal Blade   *To chop:* Place up to three handsful of nuts in the processor bowl. Process for 5 seconds continuously, then pulse until the nut fragments are of the desired size.

Metal Blade   *To pulverize:* Place the nuts in the processor bowl and process continuously, making sure that the pusher is in the feed tube.

OLIVES

Metal Blade   *To chop:* Place stoned olives in the processor bowl and pulse to the required size.

Slicing Disc   *To slice:* Only stuffed olives can be sliced. Fill the feed tube, insert the pusher and apply gentle pressure while processing. The slices are bound to be misshapen. If using for garnish choose the better-shaped rings and tuck the remainder into the mixture. Olives *must* be stoned before processing.

ONIONS

Metal Blade   *To chop:* Peel and cut into chunks, then place in the processor bowl and pulse until the required size is achieved. For fine chopping, switch on and process continuously, scraping down the sides of the bowl twice during processing.

Grating Disc   *To grate:* Cut the onions into pieces that will fit into the feed tube, insert the pusher and use firm pressure while processing. Process continuously to a thick pulp, scraping down the sides of the bowl twice during processing.

Slicing Disc   *To slice into rings:* Choose small onions and cut in half horizontally. Remove a thin slice from the top and bottom, then stack carefully into the feed tube, insert the pusher and use gentle pressure while processing. Switch off between each batch.

Slicing Disc   *To slice into strips (for salads etc. where the shape is less important):* Cut large onions into quarters which saves a lot of peeling problems. Stack in the feed tube cut-side down, insert the pusher and use medium pressure while processing. Switch off between each batch.

Metal Blade   *To purée cooked onions:* Drop through the feed tube while the motor is running. Onions that are subsequently to be used in cooked dishes can be frozen in suitable bags or containers for six to twelve months.

Treat shallots in the same way as onions.

ORANGES
See Citrus Fruits

PARMESAN
Fine Grating Disc   *To grate:* Cut off the rind and place the cheese in the feed tube against the grater. Apply firm pressure on the pusher while processing continuously. Grated Parmesan cheese can be stored in the refrigerator for several months or in the freezer. It is cheaper to buy a large piece of Parmesan and grate it yourself rather than buying the small packets. Use grated Parmesan cheese in sauces and for sprinkling over pasta dishes.

PARSLEY
See Herbs

PARSNIPS
Slicing Disc   *To slice:* For quick cooking halve or quarter the parsnips lengthways and remove the pithy core. Cut into lengths that will fit horizontally across the feed

tube. Pack the feed tube with parsnip pieces and insert the pusher, using gentle pressure while processing.

Metal Blade *To purée cooked parsnips:* Place the drained vegetables in the processor bowl, insert the pusher in the feed tube and process continuously.

PASTA

Metal Blade *To make:* Place all the pasta ingredients except the water in the food processor bowl and process to a stiff dough. While the motor is still running add the water through the feed tube. Do not add too much as dough for pasta should be firm. Continue processing until the dough forms a ball which leaves the sides of the bowl clean. If the dough is too sticky add a little flour to the bowl through the feed tube. Wrap the dough in clingfilm or put into a greased polythene bag and leave in a cool place for 30 minutes to 1 hour before rolling out. To make green pasta, chop 2 or 3 handfuls of raw spinach leaves before adding the other ingredients to the processor bowl.

PASTRY

Metal Blade *Shortcrust pastry:* Add the liquid through the feed tube as soon as the fat and flour form crumbs and while the motor is continuing to run. Process only until the mixture clings together (over-processing results in tough pastry). In traditional recipes, cut down on the recommended quantity of liquid. All pastries based on rubbing-in must be rested and chilled for 30 minutes before rolling out.

Metal Blade *Flaky pastry:* Do the rubbing-in in the processor and finish by hand.

Metal Blade *Hot-water crust:* Place the flour in the processor bowl. Add boiling fat and water mixture through the feed tube while the motor is running.

Results will be infinitely better than when made manually.

Metal Blade   *Choux pastry:* Put the flour in the processor bowl, add boiling fat and water while the motor is running and as soon as a ball is formed, drop eggs one at a time through the feed tube.

Metal Blade   *To make crumbles:* Put the flour in the processor bowl and add the butter or margarine cut into cubes. Pulse to the desired crumb texture. For sweet crumbles, remove the lid, add sugar and pulse quickly to mix in. Crumble mixes keep very well in the freezer for many months and can be spooned over fruit or stewed fruit or meat dishes for speedier cooking.

The rubbing in of fat to flour in all pastry making can always be done in the food processor. Substitute soft margarine for butter in shortcrust pastry and the dough will be mixed in a jiffy; it must then be chilled for 30 minutes before rolling out. The resulting pastry will be short and crisp. Successful results in pastry making are often marred by the addition of too much liquid. In food processor pastry the liquid is added through the feed tube during mixing and can be more carefully controlled.

PÂTÉ

Metal Blade   *To process:* Use the food processor for chopping ingredients prior to cooking and process to a paste afterwards depending on the recipe. Scrape down the sides of the bowl during processing. Many pâtés require no further cooking. Sweet pâtés served as a dessert are a delightful and unusual way to end a meal.

PEARS

Thick Slicing Disc   *To slice:* For use in fruit salads halve and core the fruit lengthwise and peel if desired. Place large fruit halves singly, upright, in the feed tube against

the slicing disc. Insert the pusher using it only to hold
the fruit in position but not to apply pressure or the fruit
will mash. Two halves of small fruit can be put into the
feed tube at the same time, cut sides towards each
other, but facing head to tail. Choose only firm fruit for
slicing. Pears discolour quickly when sliced, therefore
mix in a teaspoon of fresh lemon juice to coat the pieces
if they are to stand for any length of time.

Metal Blade   *To purée*; Chop raw pears into chunks,
place in the processor bowl and pulse to the required
consistency. To purée cooked pears place in the bowl
and process continuously.

PEPPERS

Slicing Disc   *To slice:* To obtain whole rings choose tall,
narrow rather than short, stout peppers. To de-seed
remove a thin slice from the top (stalk) end and then
use a sharp knife to cut out the seeds and extra pith in
one piece. Gently squeeze the sides of the pepper to
compress it so that it will fit into the feed tube and place
it cut side down against the slicing disc. If the pepper is
too broad to fit in in this way, slit down the full length of
one side of the vegetable and then curl it round Swiss-
roll fashion. The cut edges will be hardly detectable in
finished dishes. Insert the pusher using gentle pressure
and process each pepper separately.

Slicing Disc   *To produce curved strips:* Cut the peppers in
half vertically and remove the core and excess pith.
Nestle two or three pepper halves together and insert
vertically into the feed tube against the slicing disc.
Insert the pusher and use gentle pressure. Process each
batch separately. When peppers are required in a dish
other than for garnish, the shape is less important, but
do not place the peppers in the feed tube horizontally or
you will find that there will be a few flat slivers in among
the slices.

Metal Blade   *To chop:* First cut the seeded peppers into 2.5 cm (1 in) squares. Place in the processor bowl and pulse to the required size.

Metal Blade   *To chop roughly:* Cut the peppers into quarters and push through the feed tube while the motor is running.

Metal Blade   *To purée (raw or cooked peppers for toppings on steaks, etc.):* Add the pieces through the feed tube while the motor is running and process continuously.

Metal Blade   *To chop hot (chilli) peppers:* First blanch and remove the seeds carefully, wearing rubber gloves to prevent a burning sensation. Put the chillis in the processor bowl and pulse to the required consistency. The food processor cannot cut small items into rings.

PIZZA BASE

Metal Blade   *To make scone dough bases:* Place the flour and butter or margarine cut into cubes in the processor bowl. Place the pusher in position and process to crumbs. While the motor is running add the milk through the feed tube.

Metal Blade   *To make yeast dough bases:* Place the flour, salt and any fat in the processor bowl and process finely. Add the dissolved yeast mixture through the feed tube while the motor is still running and continue processing for 30 seconds until the dough is no longer sticky and leaves the sides of the bowl. Make up only 225 g (8 oz) flour plus other ingredients at one time as the heavy mixture tends to make the processor move about.

Metal Blade   *To make a non-yeast base:* Put wholemeal flour in the bowl and add 1 to 2 tablespoons vegetable oil, switch on the motor and add more water and ½ to 1 teaspoon salt while the motor is running. Process to a sticky dough, then remove from the processor bowl and shape into a thick pancake on a floured surface. Cook in a frying pan or hot oven.

Pizza toppings can be made with the help of a food processor. Use the slicing and grating discs to prepare the toppings.

POTATOES

To slice: Peeled or unpeeled, cooked or raw, potatoes can be sliced, using either the thin, medium or thick slicing disc. Select small potatoes that will fit easily into the feed tube or cut larger potatoes into suitable sizes. Use the thin slicing disc to make crisps.

Thick Slicing Disc *To slice raw potatoes:* Fill the feed tube with small or quartered potatoes, insert the pusher and apply medium pressure while processing. Process each batch separately. Rinse the potato slices in plenty of cold water to remove excess starch and dry between clean teatowels or kitchen paper before deep frying.

Medium Slicing Disc   Use a 5 mm (¼ in) disc for slicing raw potatoes for pommes Anna, Lyonnaise potatoes (page 240) or pommes Dauphinoise.

Thick Slicing Disc *To slice barely cooked potatoes:* Repeat as for raw but apply gentle pressure only on pusher. Use sliced cooked potatoes as toppings for meat pies, sprinkled with cheese and browned on top; or in mock moussakas or as sautéed potatoes.

Coarse Grating Disc *To shred (for potato pancakes):* Place the peeled raw potatoes cut into suitable sizes in the feed tube, insert the pusher and apply medium pressure while processing continuously one after the other. Use for Cheveux d'Ange (see page 99).

Coarse Grating Disc   *To mash:* Cooked potatoes cannot be mashed successfully in the food processor as they become waxy. Shred in the same way as raw potatoes above, then remove the disc and finish with a fork.

Chipper Disc   *To make chips:* Cut large potatoes into pieces that will fit into the feed tube and remove a slice from the base of each piece so that it fits flat against the chipper disc. Insert the pusher and use gentle pressure. Process separately in batches.

Thick Slicing Disc   *To make pommes pailles:* Trim the potatoes into blocks with a sharp knife. Place one block at a time in the feed tube, insert the pusher and use medium pressure. Remove the slices from the processor bowl and arrange the potatoes in stacks of five or six slices. Insert each stack separately into the feed tube against the disc with the thin-cut sides downwards. Insert the pusher and apply medium pressure. Process each batch separately. Rinse and dry the potato stacks before deep frying.

POULTRY

Metal Blade   *To chop raw poultry:* First remove all skin and bones, then cut the flesh into cubes. Place in the food processor bowl and pulse to the required texture.

Slicing Disc   *To slice raw poultry:* Cut into chunks that will just fit into the feed tube. Chill separately until the pieces are hard but not solid, usually 30 minutes in the freezer. Place one at a time in the feed tube against the disc. Insert the pusher and, using medium pressure, process each batch separately.

Note: The bowl, lid and blade must all be washed thoroughly before using for other food preparation. This is particularly important if you are going to process cooked meats.

Metal Blade   *To chop cold cooked poultry:* Remove skin and bones and cut the flesh into 2.5 cm (1 in) cubes. Place in the processor bowl and pulse to the required texture. Use as pancake fillings, in sauces, pâtés or any recipe requiring chopped cooked poultry.

Slicing Disc   *To shred duck (for Chinese dishes such as Crispy Duck):* This is traditionally served with a hoisin sauce and sliced spring onions (page 63) wrapped in tiny pancakes. Remove the flesh from the bone and include the skin if you prefer. Cut into large chunks that will fit smooth-side down into the feed tube and press into the tube against the blade. Insert the pusher and use medium pressure. Process each batch separately.

PRAWNS

Metal Blade   *To chop:* Place up to 100g (4 oz) shelled cooked prawns in the processor bowl and pulse until chopped to the required consistency. Shrimps should be processed similarly, but if frozen, should be thawed first to prevent them becoming mushy.

PURÉES

Metal Blade   *To purée:* Only fill the bowl to the capacity recommended by the manufacturer. Thick mixtures are less likely to overflow than thin ones. Put the ingredients into the processor bowl and process continuously, scraping down the sides of the bowl once or twice during processing. Do not remove the lid until the metal blade comes to a complete standstill.

RADISHES

Slicing Disc   *To slice:* Choose large firm radishes and remove a slice from both ends. Stack the radishes in the feed tube cut-sides down, piling them one on top of the other. Insert the pusher and, using firm pressure, process in separate batches. If not required for immediate use, keep sliced radishes in a bowl of ice-cold water.

RASPBERRIES

See Berries

RHUBARB

Coarse Slicing Disc   *To slice:* Wash the rhubarb sticks
and trim the tops and bottoms. Cut into lengths that will
fit into the feed tube and stack vertically against the
disc. Apply medium pressure on the pusher while
processing in separate batches.

Metal Blade   *To chop or purée cooked rhubarb:* Place
the fruit in the processor bowl and pulse to the required
texture. To obtain a smoother purée process continuously, scraping down the sides of the bowl once
during processing.

ROSEMARY

See Herbs

RUBBED-IN MIXTURES

Metal Blade   *To process:* Put the flour and salt or baking
powder in the processor bowl, add the fat cut into 2.5 cm
(1 in) cubes, arranging them in a circle in the bowl. Pulse
to the required texture. Insert the pusher into the feed
tube during processing to prevent spattering.

SALAD DRESSINGS

Metal Blade   *To prepare simple salad dressings for immediate use:* Place oil and vinegar or lemon juice together
with the other ingredients in the processor bowl and
process continuously, making sure that the pusher is in
the feed tube. Oil and vinegar dressings separate quite
rapidly so that no useful purpose is served if these
dressings are to be used at a later time. When other
ingredients such as garlic and herbs are to be incorporated, add these through the feed tube while the
motor is running, then follow with the oil and vinegar.
See Mayonnaise (page 127) for egg-thickened salad
dressings.

SALAMI

Slicing Disc   *To slice:* Salami may be sliced skinned or unskinned. Select widths that will fit into the feed tube. Chill the salami for 30 minutes, then cut into lengths that will fit vertically into the feed tube. It is sometimes possible to reshape salami that is slightly too big in diameter by gently pressing between the palms of the hands, but skinned salami will fall apart if this is attempted. Insert the pusher and apply gentle pressure when processing. Switch off between processing each batch.

SARDINES

Metal Blade   *To mash:* Place whole or halved sardines in the processor bowl and pulse to the required consistency. For sandwich fillings process the sardines with a little butter to make a complete sandwich spread. Remove the backbone from the sardines before processing if you wish.

SAUCES

Metal Blade   *To make emulsified sauces including eggs and fat or oil:* About 600 ml (1 pt) sauce can be made in the average-sized processor bowl. For sauces such as mayonnaise, Hollandaise, Béarnaise, etc., first put the eggs in the bowl and process until foamy, then add the liquid ingredients through the feed tube while the motor is still running.

Metal Blade   *To make flour-thickened (roux) sauces:* Place the butter or margarine and flour in the processor bowl. Process continuously until well mixed. Switch on the machine and rapidly pour in the hot liquid through the feed tube, processing until smooth. Return the mixture to the saucepan to complete cooking, stirring over medium heat.

Metal Blade   *To blend cornflour with liquid to thicken sauces:* First place the cold liquid in the food processor bowl, switch on the machine, then add the cornflour through the feed tube. When the mixture is well blended add the remaining liquid, process briefly, then pour into a saucepan and cook in the usual way.

Chop onions and other vegetables for use in sauce cookery in the processor bowl. Process soft fruits to make puréed sauces and smooth lumpy sauces by blending in the food processor. Scrape down the sides of the bowl once or twice during processing. Sauces which have become excessively lumpy and which you might normally be tempted to throw away, should be treated in this manner and any lumps that are left can be removed by pouring the mixture through a sieve into a sauce boat or bowl.

SAUSAGES
Most butchers keep sausage meat ready packeted and this will be in quantities from 225 g (8 oz) to 450 g (1 lb). If a recipe calls for a small amount of sausage meat it is probably better to use one or two sausages.

Metal Blade   *To mash:* Remove the skins (slit each sausage lengthwise with a sharp knife, then the skins will peel away easily). Place the sausage meat in the processor bowl, dividing it into four pieces. Put on the lid and pulse until mixed.

Slicing Disc   *To slice frankfurters:* Frankfurters should be chilled before slicing. Remove a thin layer from each end then cut the frankfurters into lengths which will fit vertically into the feed tube. It is essential that the feed tube is thoroughly packed widthwise, so that if you are only processing one or two it would be better first to cut each into two or four stubby chunks. Pack cut-sides down against the disc, insert the pusher and apply medium pressure while processing. Process each batch separately.

SHALLOTS
See Onions

SHRIMPS
See Prawns

SIFTING
Metal Blade *To sift and blend dry ingredients:* Place together in the processor bowl and pulse until well mixed.

SORBET
Metal Blade *To prepare:* Purée fresh soft drained canned fruit with the quantity of sugar specified in the recipe. Pour the mixture into shallow freezer containers, cover and freeze until solid but not rock hard. Remove the mixture from the freezer containers and break up into four or five pieces. Replace in the processor bowl and process only until the mixture forms a purée, about 10 seconds. Do not over-process or the mixture will become warm and the ice crystals melt which will result in a gritty sorbet. Pour the mixture back into the freezer containers and freeze until completely solid, about 12 hours. When required, remove from the freezer and leave in the refrigerator for 15 to 30 minutes to soften slightly before serving. Sorbet can be stored in the freezer for 3 to 4 months with no deterioration.

SOUP
Pre-sliced and chopped vegetables and meat will shorten soup cooking times.

Slicing Disc   Use the slicing disc when chunky soups with visible pieces are required such as a thick farmhouse vegetable soup.

Metal Blade   Use the metal blade to chop ingredients before cooking when making puréed soups. Purée again after cooking.

Soups which are to be puréed after cooking should be made thicker than usual. This will reduce the need to process in batches as stock can be added afterwards. When making large batches, cook in a minimum of liquid, so producing a bulkier highly concentrated soup. Purée in the processor bowl, then dilute with stock or water when reheated. Jiffy soups can be made by preparing a thin sauce in the processor and while it is cooking in the saucepan, finely chop vegetables or other ingredients in the processor. Pour the chopped vegetables into the sauce and continue cooking until the mixture is well blended and cooked sufficiently.

Metal Blade   *To purée large quantities:* Strain the soup into another saucepan. Place the cooked thicker pulp or pieces in the processor bowl and process continuously, scraping down the sides of the bowl once during processing. Pour the puréed mixture back into the strained liquid in the saucepan and stir thoroughly.

SPICES

Metal Blade   *To grind:* A minimum of three level tablespoons of hard berry spices such as allspice or pepper should be processed at one time. Place in the processor bowl and make sure that the pusher is in the feed tube. Then process for a few seconds, scrape down the sides of the bowl and process for a little longer. Scrape down the sides of the bowl again, lift up the metal blade and scrape away any larger fragments of spices that may have gathered, then pulse to the required texture.

Ground spices do not keep as well as whole spices and must be stored in an airtight container. Process a selection of spices together to form a blend for use in curries and Sri Lankan dishes.

SPINACH

Slicing Disc   *To shred raw for salads:* Rinse in cold water, remove the thick stems and pat the leaves dry. Pack the feed tube with spinach and, using only gentle pressure on the pusher, pulse once or twice. Repeat the process until the bowl is full, then remove the shredded spinach and continue with the next batch. If the processor bowl is over-filled or the spinach packed down too firmly, the leaves will crush.

Metal Blade   *To chop cooked spinach:* Place the drained spinach in the bowl and pulse to the required texture. Seasoning may be added during the processing.

Metal Blade   *To purée cooked spinach:* Switch on the machine and add the drained spinach through the feed tube while the motor is running. Seasoning may be added during the processing.

STRAWBERRIES
See Berries

STUFFING

Metal Blade   *To prepare:* First chop the hard ingredients. Add bread through the feed tube while the motor is still running. Sausage meat should be put in the processor bowl, then processed continuously. Raw meat should be first cut into cubes then put in the processor bowl and mixed by pulsing. Add cooked rice towards the end of processing as over-processing causes the grains to disintegrate and become slimy. Add liquids and binding ingredients such as beaten egg last.

SUET

Coarse Grating Disc *To grate:* Trim the suet and chill in the freezer until firm. Cut into pieces that will fit into the feed tube. Place one piece of suet in the feed tube, insert the pusher and, using gentle pressure, process continuously. Switch off between batches.

Metal Blade *To chop:* Chill the suet as above, then switch on the motor and drop the pieces rapidly through the feed tube into the bowl. The suet will melt if over-processed.

SUGAR

Metal Blade *To grind:* Switch on the motor and add in lumps through the feed tube while the motor is running at maximum speed. Cover the top of the feed tube with the palm of the hand to prevent spattering. Lumpy brown sugar can be treated in a similar way, but sugar balls (smooth small fragments) of a syrupy texture cannot be removed by processing. To remove these pass the sugar through a sieve, then if you wish to use the sugar balls, they must first be dissolved in water before adding to any recipe. Sugar lumps can be reduced to the size of granulated sugar and granulated sugar can be reduced to caster sugar, but the food processor cannot pulverize to the fineness of icing sugar.

SWEDES
See Turnips and Swedes

TARRAGON
See Herbs

TOMATOES

Slicing Disc *To slice:* Only small firm tomatoes can be satisfactorily sliced. Remove a sliver from the bottom of each tomato and stack in the feed tube one above the other. Use only gentle pressure on the pusher while processing. Process each batch separately. Skinned tomatoes may also be sliced but any pressure at all will cause them to disintegrate.

Metal Blade   *To chop:* Peel away the skins and put the tomatoes in the processor bowl five or six at a time. Pulse to the desired texture.

Metal Blade   *To make tomato pulp:* Add the tomatoes through the feed tube while the motor is running. If you then wish to remove the pips, the mixture must be passed through a sieve.

TURNIPS AND SWEDES

Grating Disc   *To grate:* Peel and cut into pieces that will fit into the feed tube. Place vegetable pieces in the feed tube, insert the pusher and apply medium pressure while processing continuously.

Metal Blade   *To pulp cooked swedes or turnips (to serve as a vegetable):* Place the drained cooked vegetables in the processor bowl and process continuously to the desired consistency. Scrape down the sides of the bowl once or twice during processing.

WATERCRESS

Metal Blade   *To chop:* Dry the watercress as carefully as possible between sheets of kitchen paper. Remove the stalks and place the leaves in the processor bowl. Process continuously, scraping down the sides of the bowl once during processing.

Use finely chopped watercress to flavour mayonnaise or salad dressings. Coarsely chopped watercress is a pleasant garnish for soups or for sandwich fillings. Watercress soup should be processed after cooking.

WHIPPING CREAM
See Cream

YEAST DOUGHS

Metal Blade   *To mix:* Process the dry ingredients and fat if using, before adding the yeast liquid. Add only half the liquid, then process for a few seconds before adding the remaining liquid in a thin stream. To knead the dough continue processing until it is no longer sticky. The heavy ball of dough will tend to make the food processor move about, so hold the base firmly against the worktop. Follow the manufacturer's instructions for the quantity of yeast dough that can be processed at any one time.

YOGHURT

Metal Blade   *To flavour natural yoghurts:* Put flavouring fruits and sugar in the processing bowl and process to mix. Remove the lid and spoon the yoghurt into the bowl, then pulse briefly to combine. Over-mixing will cause the yoghurt to thin. When yoghurt is to be added to soups, stews or curries, place natural yoghurt in the processor bowl and add a teaspoon of cornflour through the feed tube while the motor is running. Pour the yoghurt into the almost finished dish and bring to the boil, stirring constantly so that the cornflour has time to cook.

Recipe Section

All the recipes in the book are listed below under the usual headings of 'Pâtés and Dips', 'Starters and Light Supper Dishes', 'Soups', etc. Against each recipe you will find the section in which it appears. Turn to the front page of that section where the recipes are listed in alphabetical order.

PÂTÉS AND DIPS

AVOCADO DIP	All-in-one
BACON AND LIVER TERRINE	Fast food
COTTAGE CHEESE AND PINEAPPLE DIP	All-in-one
DANISH DIP AND DUNK	All-in-one
EGG AND ONION PÂTÉ	Combination
ICED CHEESE	Combination
LIVER PÂTÉ AND EGG DIP	All-in-one
PARTY CHEDDAR HEDGEHOG	Step-by-step
POTTED CHEESE AND HAM	All-in-one
PRAWN DIP	All-in-one
PRETZEL CHEESE PÂTÉ	All-in-one
SMOKED TROUT PÂTÉ	All-in-one
TARAMASALATA	All-in-one
TUNA PÂTÉ	All-in-one
TURKEY PÂTÉ	All-in-one

STARTERS AND LIGHT SUPPER DISHES

ALMOND RICE DARIOLES WITH PUERTO RICAN SAUCE	Combination
CHEESE SOUFFLÉ	Step-by-step
CRAB AND EGG STUFFED TOMATOES	All-in-one
GREEN VELVET TERRINE	All-in-one
INDIVIDUAL ONION QUICHES	Combination

SOUPS

MAIN DISHES

MEAT

PEANUT COATED HAMBURGERS IN
   TOMATO SAUCE   Step-by-step
PORK CHOPS PEIRCEY   Step-by-step
SIMPLE MOUSSAKA   Combination
STEAK AND KIDNEY PUDDING   Fast food
STEAK DIANE   Step-by-step
STUFFED MARROW   Step-by-step
STUFFED SPANISH ONIONS   Step-by-step
SWEET PICKLE AND OLIVE MINCED BEEF
   LOAF   All-in-one
UNSOPHISTICATED LAMB CURRY   Combination

FISH
FISH CROQUETTES   All-in-one
PLAICE FILLETS IN ORANGE AND ONION
   SAUCE   Step-by-step
SCALLOPS IN SAFFRON LEMON AND
   GARLIC SAUCE   Fast food
TUNA LOAF   All-in-one

POULTRY
BREAST OF CHICKEN SAUCE
   CHAMPIGNONS   Combination
CHICKEN CASSEROLE WITH APPLES AND
   PEPPERS   All-in-one
CHICKEN MAYONNAISE SALAD   Fast food
CHICKEN PAPRIKA   Combination
COUNTRY STYLE CHICKEN   Fast food

VEGETABLES
CHEVEUX D'ANGE   All-in-one
COURGETTES JARDINIÈRES   All-in-one
LYONNAISE POTATOES   Fast food
MAYFAIR CARROTS   Step-by-step
PIPERADE   Step-by-step
SAUTÉED MUSHROOMS   Combination

SAUTÉED POTATO SLICES   All-in-one
VEGETABLE CUTLETS   All-in-one

SALADS
CARROT AND ORANGE SALAD   Combination
CELERY AND CARROT MUSTARD CREAM
   SALAD   Combination
MARINATED CUCUMBER   All-in-one
PIQUANT TOMATO SALAD   All-in-one
TOMATO AND ONION SALAD   Combination
WALDORF SALAD   All-in-one
WALNUT AND CELERY SLAW   All-in-one

SAUCES AND SALAD DRESSINGS
BÉCHAMEL SAUCE   Step-by-step
EGG AND ANCHOVY SAUCE   Combination
FRENCH DRESSING   All-in-one
GARLIC ALMOND AND PINE NUT SALAD
   DRESSING   All-in-one
MAYONNAISE   All-in-one
POULETTE SAUCE   All-in-one
SAUCE ÉSPAGNOLE   Step-by-step
SAUTÉED ONION PURÉE   Step-by-step
SAVOURY FISH BUTTER   All-in-one
SIMPLE WHITE SAUCE   All-in-one
TARRAGON VINAIGRETTE   All-in-one
TOMATO AND HONEY SALAD DRESSING   All-in-one
TOMATO SAUCE   All-in-one
WHITE SAUCE SUITABLE FOR COATING   Step-by-step

PUDDINGS AND DESSERTS
BANANA AND SULTANA PÂTÉ   All-in-one
BLACKBERRY AND BANANA CRISP   All-in-one
BLACKBERRY PUD   Fast Food
CARROTTY PIE   Step-by-step
CHOCOLATE HAZELNUT PÂTÉ   All-in-one

CHRISTMAS PUDDING	Fast Food
DEWY FRUIT SALAD	Step-by-step
HAPPY PUDDING	All-in-one
NORMANDY DEEP APPLE PANCAKE	Step-by-step
RASPBERRY ICE CREAM	Fast food
RHUBARB AND APPLE COBBLER	Step-by-step
RHUBARB SUET PUDDING	Step-by-step
THATCHED GOOSEBERRY PIE	All-in-one
WHIZZ OF FRUIT DESSERT	All-in-one

CAKES, BISCUITS AND BREAD

ALMOND CAKES	Step-by-step
ALMOND AND LEMON LOAF CAKE	Step-by-step
AMERICAN CHOCOLATE SPICED SHEET CAKE	All-in-one
BREAD	All-in-one
CHERRY AND CASHEW NUT TEA BREAD	All-in-one
CROISSANTS	All-in-one
CRUSTY HERBY FRENCH BREAD	Combination
CRUSTY WALNUT PULL LOAF	Combination
CYPRUS CAKE	Combination
EASY CHOCOLATE ICING	All-in-one
GINGERBREAD MEN	All-in-one
HAZELNUT COFFEE CAKE	All-in-one
HOME FARM SHEET CAKE	All-in-one
HONIGEN FRUIT LOAF	All-in-one
INMACULADA'S COOKIES	Combination
IRRESISTIBLE CRISPS	All-in-one
MARMALADE CAKES	All-in-one
NEW ENGLAND LAYER CAKE	Combination
PINEAPPLE CAKE	All-in-one
PIZZA SCONE BASE	All-in-one
PLAIN SCONES	All-in-one
RUMBLES	All-in-one
SATSUMA MADEIRA CAKE	All-in-one
SCOTCH SHORTBREAD	All-in-one

SUNSET CHERRY LOGS — All-in-one
VICTORIA SANDWICH (QUICK MIX) — All-in-one
VICTORIA SANDWICH (TRADITIONAL) — All-in-one

PASTRY

CHOUX PASTRY — Step-by-step
HOME-MADE PASTA — All-in-one
SAVOURY STUFFED CHOUX BUNS — Step-by-step
SHORTCRUST PASTRY — All-in-one
WHOLEWHEAT SCONES — All-in-one

PRESERVES, PICKLES AND CHUTNEYS

APPLE CHUTNEY — All-in-one
AUBERGINE PICKLE — All-in-one
HONEY AND BANANA FRUIT CURD — All-in-one
LEMON CURD — Fast food
FAT-FREE MINCEMEAT — All-in-one
RASPBERRY CURD — Fast food

STUFFINGS AND DUMPLINGS, MISCELLANEOUS

BACON PIZZA TOPPING — Combination
FRUIT STUFFING — Combination
LEMON BRANDY BUTTER — All-in-one
MUSHROOM DUXELLES — All-in-one
PLAIN DUMPLINGS — All-in-one
RICOTTA FILLING FOR PASTA — All-in-one

DRINKS

BLOODY MARY — All-in-one
JOGGER'S LIQUID BREAKFAST — All-in-one
NON-ALCOHOLIC PARTY PUNCH — All-in-one

ALL-IN-ONE RECIPES

This section is the one to start with, particularly if you are not familiar with the ins and outs of how the processor works. You need think no further than collecting the ingredients together; the mixing will be practically instant. Further cooking is of the simplest kind; washing up is drastically reduced; and the pages in this part of the book will, I am sure, be well thumbed.

As preparation in the food processor is so fast it is a good idea to light or switch on the oven before starting if the dishes are to be baked in a hot oven – then you won't have to wait while it heats up. When recommended temperatures are 180°C (350°F) Gas Mark 4 a pre-heat is less important.

AMERICAN CHOCOLATE SHEET CAKE

Sheet cakes are baked in a Swiss roll or shallow baking tin. The cakes rise to about 2.5 cm (1 in) thickness. When cooked, cut the cake into squares or fingers and ice if you wish.

100 g (4 oz) butter   METAL BLADE
225 g (8 oz) soft dark brown sugar
2.5 ml (½ tsp) salt
5 ml (1 tsp) bicarbonate of soda
2.5 ml (½ tsp) cinnamon
1.25 ml (¼ tsp) ground cloves
5 ml (1 tsp) vanilla essence
150 ml (¼ pt) natural yoghurt
50g (2 oz) cocoa
2 size-2 eggs, lightly beaten
200 g (7 oz) plain flour, sifted

Grease the sides of a Swiss roll tin measuring approximately 34 × 24 cm (13 × 9 in) and line the base with non-stick or greaseproof paper. If you are using greaseproof paper grease both sides. Cut the butter into about eight pieces and place in a circle in the bowl. Add the sugar and process until the mixture is fluffy. Scrape down the sides of the bowl, add the salt, bicarbonate of soda, cinnamon, cloves, vanilla essence, yoghurt and cocoa and process until the mixture is well blended. While the motor is running pour in the eggs through the feed tube and when these are beaten in (about 15 seconds), switch off the machine. Remove the lid, sprinkle about half the flour evenly over the surface of the mixture and replace the lid and pulse once of twice until the flour disappears from view. Add the remaining flour in the same way, then pulse again briefly.

The mixture should now resemble dark heavy sticky

batter. Pour the cake batter into the tin and level with a palette knife. Bake in the centre of a moderately hot oven, 190°C (375°F) Gas Mark 5, for 20 to 25 minutes, or until the top of the cake is shiny and resilient to the touch. Remove the cake from the oven and leave to cool in the tin before cutting into squares. The cake will freeze well either before or after cutting.

Makes 30 pieces.

APPLE CHUTNEY

Chutneys should be cooked in a heavy-based saucepan over gentle heat to discourage the mixture from sticking. This recipe contains no added sugar, relying entirely upon the dates for sweetening. Have a trial to see how you like it and then if you wish, increase the quantities but the ingredients will have to be processed in batches.

225 g (8 oz) cooking apples, peeled,   METAL BLADE
   cored and quartered
1 medium onion, peeled and halved
75 g (3 oz) stoned dates
2.5 ml (½ tsp) ground ginger
2.5 ml (½ tsp) ground allspice
Pinch Cayenne pepper
200 ml (7 fl oz) malt vinegar

Switch on the machine and while the motor is running add the apples, onion, dates, spices and Cayenne and 2 or 3 tablespoons of the vinegar through the feed tube. Process until the mixture is finely chopped, scraping down the sides of the bowl twice. Turn the mixture into a heavy-based saucepan, bring to the boil, then reduce the heat and simmer gently, stirring frequently, for about 40 minutes or until the mixture is thick and all the vinegar has been absorbed. Leave to cool, then spoon the chutney into prepared jars. Cover each with a waxed disc and a jam-pot cover.

Makes 1 to 2 jars

AUBERGINE PICKLE

Make sure that you buy unblemished aubergines with shiny skins and choose them long and slim rather than short and fat.

450 g (1 lb) aubergines   SLICING DISC
Salt
1 clove garlic, peeled and halved
1 dried red chilli pepper
100 ml (7 tbsp) red wine vinegar
150 ml (¼ pt) olive oil

Wash the aubergines but do not peel. Remove the stalk ends; cut the aubergines in half lengthwise then cut each piece into two also lengthwise. Hold the aubergine as upright as possible in the feed tube and slice. Put the aubergine slices in a colander over a bowl or plate and stir in 1 tbsp of salt. Cover and leave for about 2 hours until dark juices appear on the surface of the slices. Drain thoroughly. Put the vinegar and about 225 ml (8 fl oz) water into a large saucepan and bring to the boil. Add the aubergine, then reduce the heat and simmer for 3 to 4 minutes. Drain thoroughly, then wrap in a clean teacloth and leave until the aubergine slices are completely dry. They will be soft and of a dark colour. Pack the cut aubergines, garlic and chilli pepper into one 900 g (2 lb) or two 450 g (1 lb) glass jars and fill with the oil, making sure that the latter just covers the aubergines. Cover with a waxed disc or piece of clingfilm and screw the top on securely. Leave for four weeks before using, shaking the jar occasionally. Serve with cold meats.

Makes 1 to 2 jars

AVOCADO DIP

This is a really lovely dip to serve with deep-fried breaded scampi to start off a dinner party. You can also serve it as an ordinary dip to go with mild-flavoured vegetables such as cauliflower and carrot or with naccho chips.

2 ripe avocados ·   METAL BLADE
60 ml (4 tbsp) good quality mayonnaise
Juice of 1 small lemon
Shake garlic salt
1.25 ml (¼ tsp) Cayenne pepper
Salt
Pepper } to taste

Peel the avocados and cut the flesh into four or six pieces. Put in the processor bowl with the mayonnaise, lemon juice, garlic powder and Cayenne pepper and process until just smooth. Season to taste with salt and pepper and pour into a serving bowl. Set aside for 2 hours before serving.

To serve place the bowl on a large dish surrounded by freshly fried breaded scampi and provide a supply of cocktail sticks for the guests to use.

Makes ½ pt (300 ml)

BANANA AND SULTANA PÂTÉ

Surprise your family and guests by serving a sweet pâté for dessert. Offer ice cream wafers, rich tea or petit beurre biscuits and arrange sliced kiwi fruit, grapes or drained sliced canned lychees around the edges of the plate.

   1 large banana   METAL BLADE
   50 g (2 oz) unsalted butter
   15 ml (1 tbsp) golden syrup
   25 g (1 oz) washed sultanas
   5 ml (1 tsp) lemon juice

Peel the banana, cut into three pieces, put into the processor bowl and process until mashed. While the motor is running add the butter, cut into three or four pieces, through the feed tube. When the mixture is smooth add the syrup, sultanas and lemon juice. Process until the sultanas are finely chopped, scraping down the sides of the bowl twice during processing. Spoon into a small pâté dish and refrigerate for 30 minutes before serving. The pâté keeps well for two or three days in the refrigerator.

Serves 3 to 4

BLACKBERRY AND BANANA CRISP

Blackberries and bananas go together very well but fresh blackberries may not always be obtainable. Frozen berries will do just as well and you can substitute blackcurrants or raspberries – even apple slices complement the bananas. To save extra washing-up melt the butter or margarine in the pie dish while the oven is heating but take care when handling the hot dish.

   75 g (3 oz) butter or margarine   METAL BLADE
   175 g (6 oz) wholemeal bread, crusts removed
   50 g (2 oz) demerara sugar
   2.5 ml (½ tsp) mixed ground spice

225 g (8 oz) blackberries, frozen or fresh
2 large bananas
25 g (1 oz) sugar

Preheat the oven to moderately hot 190°C (375°F) Gas Mark 5 and while it is heating, melt the butter or margarine in a pie dish. Attach the metal blade and switch on the food processor. While the motor is running add the bread, already torn into pieces. When the bread has turned into crumbs add the demerara sugar and the mixed spice and pour the melted butter or margarine in through the feed tube. Process only until the bread is coated with the butter but not drawn together in one lump. Peel and slice the bananas (it is easiest to do this by hand) and layer the bananas and blackberries with the caster sugar in the pie dish in which you melted the butter. Spoon the bread mixture over the fruit but do not press down. Bake in the preheated oven for 15 to 25 minutes or until the top is crisp and the fruit is piping hot. Serve immediately.

Serves 4

BLOODY MARY

The drink seems innocuous enough but provides quite a punch, so reduce the quantity of vodka drastically if you are the driver.

300 ml (½ pt) canned tomato juice   METAL BLADE
5 ml (1 tsp) Worcestershire sauce
15 ml (1 tbsp) fresh lemon juice
Dash Tabasco
60 ml (2 fl oz) vodka
2 ice cubes

Put all the ingredients in the processor bowl. Make sure that the pusher is in the feed tube, then process for 30 seconds. Pour into a jug or individual wine glasses and provide extra ice cubes.

Serves 3 to 4

BREAD

Provided you follow the manufacturer's instructions as to the weight of dough that can be mixed in your food pcocessor, you can follow any bread recipe. To save all the kneading and 'knocking back', I include a pinch of Vitamin C powder (you can buy Vitamin C in either tablet or powder form), and I also use the easy blend dried yeast. At the time of writing I could only obtain Homepride Harvest Gold, but there may well be other similar products in the future. The yeast needs no pre-mixing and if you have been hesitant about making bread, try this speedy food processor method which is always successful for me.

225 g (8 oz) plain flour   METAL BLADE
2.5 ml (½ tsp) salt
1.25 ml (¼ tsp) sugar
⅓ sachet easy blend dried yeast
Pinch Vitamin C powder
25g (1 oz) butter or margarine, softened
Approx. 150 ml (¼ pt) lukewarm water

Put the flour, salt, sugar, yeast and Vitamin C powder into the processor bowl and process for 10 seconds to sift. Remove the lid, add the butter or margarine and process until it is thoroughly rubbed in. While the machine is running pour in the water through the feed tube and process for 1 minute or until the dough is smooth and no longer sticky and draws away from the sides of the bowl. Remove the blade from the bowl, take out the dough, shape on a lightly floured work surface, then press into a well-greased 450 g (1 lb) loaf tin. Put the tin into a large polythene bag, seal the bag at the top and leave in a warm place for about 1 hour or until the dough has risen to the top of the tin.

Preheat the oven to very hot 230°C (450°F) Gas Mark 8 and bake the loaf for 25 to 35 minutes or until well risen and brown on top. Remove from the oven and turn out the loaf. Tap the base with your knuckles and if the bread is cooked, it will sound hollow. Should the bread require further baking, put it on a greased baking tray in a very hot oven for about 10 minutes. Remove the loaf from the tin or tray and cool on a wire rack – although it is scrumptious when served hot, straight from the oven.

Makes one 450 g/1 lb loaf

BRUSSELS SPROUTS SOUP

Don't be put off by the thought of using Brussels sprouts in soup. The taste is delicate and similar to a smooth spinach, watercress or cucumber soup. The soup tends to thicken during standing time so if you are keeping it for more than a few hours, thin it down with more stock.

450 g (1 lb) Brussels sprouts, washed   METAL BLADE
   and trimmed
1 small onion, peeled and cut into quarters
1.1 litre (2 pt) well-flavoured chicken stock
45 ml (3 tbsp) vegetable oil (not olive)
90 ml (6 tbsp) plain flour
300 ml (½ pt) milk
Salt
Pepper

In a large saucepan cook the Brussels sprouts and the onion in the stock until the onion is soft. Put the oil, flour and milk in the processor bowl and process until smooth. Remove the lid and, using a slotted spoon, add the sprouts and the onion, leaving the stock in the saucepan. Process to a thick purée, scraping down the sides of the bowl once. Pour the purée back into the stock, bring to the boil, reduce the heat and cook gently for 10 minutes. Stir constantly during cooking to prevent the soup from forming lumps on the bottom of the pan. Season to taste with salt and pepper although if the stock is well seasoned, this may not be necessary. Serve hot.

Serves 8

CHERRY AND CASHEW NUT TEA BREAD

Cashew nuts have a soft bland flavour and texture but you can substitute flaked almonds if you prefer.

75 g (3 oz) cashew nuts	METAL BLADE

225 g (8 oz) self-raising flour
100 g (4 oz) glacé cherries
5 ml (1 tsp) grated nutmeg
5 ml (1 tsp) ground mixed spice
100 g (4 oz) soft margarine or softened butter
100 g (4 oz) dark soft brown sugar
2 size-2 eggs
2.5 ml (½ tsp) bicarbonate of soda
120 ml (4 fl oz) milk
15 ml (1 tbsp) black treacle

Put the cashew nuts, one tablespoon of the flour and all the cherries into the processor bowl. Insert the pusher in the feed tube and process until the nuts and cherries are roughly chopped, scraping down the sides of the bowl once. Remove the lid, add the remaining flour and the spices and process until these are all mixed in. Remove the lid once more and add the remaining ingredients. Process until well blended, then pour the mixture into a greased and lined 1 kg (2 lb) loaf tin and bake in a moderate oven, 180°C (350°F) Gas Mark 4, for 50 minutes to 1 hour or until the loaf is well risen, brown on top and resilient to the touch. If during cooking the loaf becomes too brown, cover with a piece of greaseproof paper or foil.

Makes 1 × 1 kg (2 lb) tea bread

CHEVEUX D'ANGE

Serve these potato wisps as a cocktail snack, a garnish for soups or an accompaniment to meat dishes. The quantities are unimportant since you can make as many or as few as you like. Cooking takes some time as only a few can be fried at one time.

Potatoes, peeled and quartered	COARSE SHREDDING
Oil for deep frying	OR JULIENNE DISC

Before processing drain the potatoes thoroughly and press them between sheets of kitchen paper or a folded teacloth to remove any excess moisture. Coarsely grate the potatoes into the processor bowl, then remove and pat dry once more. Heat the oil to 190°C (375°F) and carefully fry the potato shreds a few at a time, removing them with a slotted spoon and draining them on kitchen paper. Repeat until you have fried all the potatoes. (Because the potato wisps fry so quickly you may need to reduce the heat during cooking.)

225 g (8 oz) raw potatoes serves 6

CHICKEN CASSEROLE WITH APPLES AND PEPPERS

Use either a whole roasting chicken and cut it up yourself, or buy chicken joints.

1 onion, peeled and halved   SLICING DISC
1 large red pepper, halved, cored and deseeded
1 medium green pepper, halved, cored and deseeded
30 ml (2 tbsp) oil
8 chicken joints, skinned
10 ml (2 tsp) cornflour
450 ml (¾ pt) sweet white wine
150 ml (¼ pt) water
Salt
Pepper
225 g (8 oz) dessert apples

Process the onion, red pepper and green pepper into slices. Heat the oil in a large flameproof casserole and brown the chicken joints on all sides. Stir in the vegetable slices, cornflour, wine and water and season to taste with salt and pepper. Reduce the heat under the casserole. Peel, quarter and core the apples and slice in the food processor. Spread the apple slices over the chicken pieces and baste with the sauce. Cover the casserole with the lid and cook gently for 1 to 1¼ hours until the chicken flesh is tender and comes easily away from the bone. Stir from time to time during cooking to prevent the vegetables from burning. Add a few tablespoons of water if the sauce seems to be drying up too much. Serve hot directly from the casserole.

Serves 6

CHINESE STIR-FRIED BEEF

To obtain really thin slices of beef, it is best to start with a whole piece – a joint is easiest to cope with. Remove the fatty wrapping and all the pieces of string and cut the joint lengthwise along the grain into blocks that will fit into the feed tube. Before slicing, chill these blocks in the freezer for about 1 hour.

700 g (1½ lb) lean topside of beef   SLICING DISC
1 large green pepper, halved, cored and deseeded
1 large red pepper, halved, cored and deseeded
3 medium onions, peeled
45 ml (3 tbsp) vegetable oil
30 ml (2 tbsp) sesame seeds
10 ml (2 tsp) cornflour
2.5 ml (½ tsp) salt
45 ml (3 tbsp) soy sauce
2.5 ml (½ tsp) ground black pepper
1.25 ml (¼ tsp) ground ginger
45 ml (3 tbsp) sherry
150 ml (¼ pt) cold water

Attach the slicing disc, place a block of meat in the feed tube and secure the lid. Insert the pusher into the tube, then switch on and process into slices. Switch off, remove the slices, repeat the process until all the meat has been sliced. Fill the feed tube with peppers and process into slices, then process the onions. (It may be necessary to empty the processor bowl after half the vegetables have been sliced.)

Heat the oil in a large heavy-based frying pan and add the sesame seeds. As soon as these begin to jump about add the meat, peppers and onions, a handful at a time. Stir briskly with a wooden spoon between each addition. Now add the cornflour, salt, soy sauce, pepper, ginger, sherry and water and stir thoroughly. Cover with a lid, reduce the heat and cook gently for about 10 minutes, stirring occasionally. Serve with freshly boiled rice.

Serves 6

CHOCOLATE HAZELNUT PÂTÉ

This is a rich pâté which goes a long way. The shelled hazelnuts must be roasted or toasted until the skins can be rubbed off. When these have been discarded roast or toast the nuts again until they are a light brown colour. The hazelnuts are the predominant flavour in this pâté.

25 g (1 oz) plain dessert chocolate   METAL BLADE
   (Bourneville or similar)
50 g (2 oz) skinned toasted hazelnuts
100 g (4 oz) unsalted butter, at room temperature

Break up the chocolate into squares, put into the processor bowl and process continuously until finely chopped. While the motor is still running add the hazelnuts and process until very finely chopped. Insert the pusher in the feed tube during chopping. Remove the lid, scrape down the sides of the bowl and if necessary remove the metal blade and scrape out any chocolate that may have lodged underneath it. Replace the blade carefully, add the butter cut into four pieces, then process until smooth. Spoon the mixture into a pâté dish or small ramekin dishes and refrigerate. The pâté hardens after about 1 hour in the refrigerator, but may be stored there for 4 to 5 days. To soften for easy spreading remove the pâté from the refrigerator 15 minutes before it is required.

Serves 6 to 8

CORNED BEEF PATTIES

Very quickly made, these patties can also be cooked in the microwave oven using the browning dish.

1 × 340 g (12 oz) can corned beef   METAL BLADE
½ green pepper, deseeded
90 ml (6 tbsp) dried breadcrumbs
75 ml (5 tbsp) mayonnaise
1 egg
5 ml (1 tsp) mustard powder
1.25 ml (¼ tsp) salt
1.25 ml (¼ tsp) black pepper

For frying:
Flour
Butter or oil

Cut the corned beef into about four pieces and place in the processor bowl. Switch on the machine and while the motor is still running, add through the feed tube the green pepper, cut into two pieces, then add all the remaining ingredients and process until they are well mixed. Remove the mixture from the bowl, divide into six portions and shape into patties 6.5 × 1.5 cm (2½ × ¾ in).

Lightly dust each patty with flour and shallow fry them in butter or oil for about 3 minutes, turning the patties over as soon as the underside is brown. Remove from the pan, drain on kitchen paper and serve.

Makes 8

COTTAGE CHEESE AND PINEAPPLE DIP

You can use canned pineapple but I prefer the fresh variety using up the remainder in fruit salad.

1 × 2.5 cm (1 in) thick slice of   METAL BLADE
   juicy pineapple
225 g (8 oz) unflavoured cottage cheese
50 g (2 oz) butter at room temperature

Cut the pineapple into five or six pieces. Switch on the
machine and while the motor is running drop the pineapple through the feed tube. As soon as the fruit is finely
chopped, switch off, remove the lid and add the cottage
cheese and the butter. Process until the mixture is well
blended and no obvious cottage cheese curds are visible.
Scrape down the sides of the bowl once or twice during
processing. Spoon the dip into a small serving dish, cover
and chill for 1 hour before serving.

Makes about 300 ml (½ pt)

COUNTRY SPINACH SOUP

This is a thick soup relying almost entirely upon fresh
spinach for its flavour and texture so that it is plain and
wholesome. If you prefer a thinner soup, extra water or
milk can be added towards the end of the cooking time.

700 ml (1¼ pt) milk   METAL BLADE
50 g (2 oz) butter or margarine
900 g (2 lb) fresh spinach, thoroughly washed and
   stems removed
15 g (½ oz) cornflour
Salt
Pepper
1.25 ml (¼ tsp) grated nutmeg

Put 600 ml (1 pt) milk and the butter or margarine into a
large saucepan and heat gently to warm the milk and melt
the fat. Meanwhile put one-quarter of the spinach leaves

in the processor bowl and process until finely chopped. Stir into the milk mixture. Process the remaining spinach in batches and add each to the pan. Add 600 ml (1 pt) water and raise the heat. Bring to the boil, stirring continuously. Reduce the heat and simmer for 20 to 30 minutes or until the spinach is cooked and the soup thickens. Blend the cornflour with the remaining milk, stir into the soup and bring back to the boil. Season to taste with salt and pepper and stir in the nutmeg.

Serves 6 to 8

COURGETTES JARDINIÈRES

Ideally you should use fresh herbs in this recipe but if you are unable to obtain these, use about one-third the amount stated of dried herbs.

4 medium courgettes, washed, topped   SLICING DISC
   and tailed, but not peeled
30 ml (2 tbsp) freshly chopped parsley (page 57)
5 ml (1 tsp) tarragon leaves
10 ml (2 tsp) freshly chopped chives
5 ml (1 tsp) thyme leaves
15 ml (1 tbsp) fresh lemon juice
Walnut-sized piece butter
1 clove garlic, crushed with a little salt

Cut the courgettes into lengths that will fit upright in the feed tube. Put in one or two at a time, insert the pusher and apply medium pressure. Switch on the machine and process the courgettes in batches, switching off the machine between each batch. Put the remaining ingredients into a saucepan and heat, stirring constantly, until the butter melts. Add the courgettes and 60 ml (4 tbsp) hot water. Cover the pan with the lid and simmer for 8 to

12 minutes, or until the courgettes are just tender. Taste and add salt if needed. If only 2 tablespoons of liquid remain, the courgettes can be served up in this, but if there is more liquid than this, remove the courgettes to a warmed dish using a slotted spoon and fast boil the liquid until it is reduced to 30 ml (2 tbsp), then pour over the vegetables. Serve hot or cold.

Serves 4 to 6

CRAB AND EGG STUFFED TOMATOES

If you are looking for something different in the way of a low calorie starter, try this one. Only 35 calories for each stuffed tomato.

20 firm small tomatoes   METAL BLADE
1 × 189 g (6½ oz) can crab meat, drained
4 eggs, hard-boiled, shelled
15 ml (1 tbsp) good quality mayonnaise
Lettuce leaves

Wash and dry the tomatoes. Remove and reserve a slice from the round end of each tomato. Scoop the pulp out of the tomatoes and keep for use in soups. Halve the eggs and put into the processor bowl with the drained crab meat and mayonnaise. Pulse six to eight times until the egg and crab meat are finely chopped but not processed to a paste. Generously fill the tomatoes with the mixture, allowing it to peek about 1 cm (½ in) above the rims. Top with the reserved tomato lids and arrange on a platter of lettuce leaves.

Makes 20

CROISSANTS

Making traditional croissants is slow because the butter has to be added during the rolling and folding process. This is a quick-mix recipe where all the ingredients are added at one time. After chilling, roll and shape the dough, then bake at once or, if it is more convenient, refrigerate the uncooked croissants until you are ready to pop them into a hot oven and serve freshly baked. The dough can be stored in the freezer for about 1 month.

350 g (12 oz) strong white flour   METAL BLADE
5 ml (1 tsp) sugar
5 ml (1 tsp) salt
1 × 6 g (¼ oz) packet easy blend dried yeast
250 g (9 oz) butter, refrigerator hard
Approx. 200 ml (⅓ pt) lukewarm water

For brushing:
Beaten egg

Put the flour into the processor bowl and add the sugar, salt and yeast. Switch on the machine and while the motor is running, drop 25 g (1 oz) of the butter cut into two or three pieces and most of the water in through the feed tube. Process until a sticky dough is formed. Remove the lid and arrange the remaining butter cut into 2.5 cm (1 in) cubes over the surface of the dough. Pulse until the butter is mixed in but still lumpy. Remove the dough from the bowl, shape into a ball on a floured surface, then wrap in greased polythene and chill for several hours.

Remove the dough from the refrigerator, cut in half and roll each piece separately into a long strip on a floured board. Fold over each strip in three, roll to a long strip and fold into three again. Roll out the dough to the thickness of a 10p piece and cut into 15 cm (4 in) squares.

Gather the trimmings together and refrigerate these before re-rolling and shaping. Roll up each square diagonally from one corner and curve into a crescent shape.

Place the croissants on to greased baking trays and brush the tops with beaten egg. Leave to stand at room temperature for about 30 minutes or until the croissants are puffy. Preheat the oven to hot 200°C (400°F) Gas Mark 6 and bake the croissants for 30 minutes or until they are golden brown and sound hollow when tapped underneath. Serve warm with butter.

Makes 12 to 16

DANISH DIP AND DUNK

Serve as a starter with drinks before a special dinner or on a buffet table. The quantity can be increased.

120 ml (4 fl oz) corn or sunflower oil   METAL BLADE
75 ml (5 tbsp) fresh lemon juice
10 ml (2 tsp) caster sugar
5 ml (1 tsp) paprika
100 g (4 oz) Danish Blue cheese, broken up

Bite-sized raw vegetables including carrots,
    cauliflower and celery

Switch on the machine and while the motor is running add through the feed tube all the ingredients except the vegetables in the listed order. Process until smooth, scraping down the sides of the bowl once. Pour the dip into a serving bowl and place in the centre of a large dish surrounded by the cut-up raw vegetables.

Makes 350 ml (½ pt); serves 6 to 8

EASY CHOCOLATE ICING

An easy soft chocolate icing to top or sandwich a cake.

> 150 g (5 oz) icing sugar, sieved   METAL BLADE
> 50 g (2 oz) butter at room temperature
> 10 ml (2 tsp) milk
> 30 ml (2 tbsp) drinking chocolate powder

Put the icing sugar into the processor bowl, add the butter cut into four or six pieces, the milk and the chocolate powder. Insert the pusher in the feed tube, then process until a soft smooth icing is formed, scraping down the sides of the bowl once. This icing can be stored in the freezer or refrigerator but should be beaten again until soft before using.

Sufficient to fill or ice 1 average cake

FAT-FREE MINCEMEAT

A mincemeat without the greasy texture of suet. The quantity is right for the average food processor bowl. If you wish to increase the recipe, process each batch separately. Larger capacity bowls can cope easily with a double quantity. The ingredients must be processed in the order given to prevent the mincemeat becoming mushy.

> 100 g (4 oz) cooking apple, weighed   METAL BLADE
>   after peeling and coring
> 100 g (4 oz) currants
> 25 g (1 oz) chopped candied peel
> 100 g (4 oz) seedless raisins
> 50 g (2 oz) sultanas
> 50 g (2 oz) (10) glacé cherries, washed
> 50 g (2 oz) whole almonds, blanched and skinned

15 ml (1 tbsp) fresh lemon juice
2.5 ml (½ tsp) ground mixed spice
100 g (4 oz) dark soft brown sugar
30 ml (2 tbsp) brandy

Quarter the apple, put into the processor bowl and pulse until the apple is well chopped. Remove the lid and add the currants, peel, raisins, sultanas, cherries and almonds. Process in 5 second bursts until the almonds appear to be chopped. Then add the lemon juice through the feed tube and process for 1 or 2 seconds to mix. Remove the lid and add the spice and sugar, then pulse until these ingredients are well incorporated and no specks of dry sugar are visible. Remove the lid, sprinkle the brandy over the surface of the chopped fruit and pulse three or four times to mix in the brandy. Spoon the mincemeat into a dry sterilized 450 g (1 lb) jar, pressing the mixture well down. Cover with a jam pot cover or clingfilm and refrigerate for not less than 1 month and not more than 6 months. The mincemeat can also be stored in the freezer.

Makes 450 g (1 lb)

FISH CROQUETTES

You don't need to rely on the fishmonger for the fish for these easy croquettes. I find the frozen cod or haddock portions just as good for this recipe. I also use left-over boiled rice and if the cheese is ready grated, it will save you changing the processor attachment. For those who cannot eat fried food the croquettes can be poached in lightly salted water and the length of cooking time will be similar.

50 g (2 oz) hard cheese, Cheddar   GRATING DISC
   or similar   METAL BLADE
400 to 450 g (14 to 16 oz) white fish,
   without skin or bones
30 ml (2 tbsp) flour
30 ml (2 tbsp) vegetable oil
45 ml (3 tbsp) milk
2.5 ml (½ tsp) salt
1.25 ml (¼ tsp) ground white pepper
1.25 ml (¼ tsp) paprika
100 g (4 oz) cooked rice

For frying:
Oil

Attach the grating disc and process the cheese. Leaving
the cheese in the bowl, remove the disc and attach the
metal blade. Switch on the motor and add the fish through
the feed tube, followed by the flour, oil, milk and
seasonings. As soon as the mixture is well blended,
remove the lid and add the rice. Pulse only until the rice is
incorporated.

Turn the mixture out on to a wet surface and divide into
ten pieces. Shape into croquettes either with wet hands or
on a floured board. Heat about 4 cm (1½ in) vegetable oil
in a large saucepan or frying pan to about 180°C (360°F) or
until a cube of bread will turn golden brown in 50 to 60
seconds. Fry the croquettes, turning them over as soon as
they are brown underneath. (If the oil is too hot and the
croquettes turn dark brown very quickly, it could mean
that the fish inside will still be raw, so do lower the heat if
you find it necessary.) The croquettes take 4 to 5 minutes
to cook. Drain on kitchen paper and serve hot or cold.

Serves 3 to 4

FRENCH DRESSING

French dressing is easy to mix in a wide-necked screw-topped jar. It is extremely difficult to combine the ingredients in a vinegar bottle because of the narrow aperture and seasonings or herbs get stuck around the opening. Make sure that jar and bottle lids are secure before shaking them to mix the dressing. Basic French dressing made in the food processor is well blended and ready for immediate use; herbed dressings are better when made in the food processor because the herbs can be chopped at the same time. The following ingredients are for basic French dressing.

90 ml (6 tbsp) vegetable oil   METAL BLADE
30 ml (2 tbsp) wine vinegar
2.5 ml (½ tsp) salt
10 ml (2 tsp) caster sugar

Put all the ingredients into the processor bowl, insert the pusher in the feed tube and process at maximum speed. Store and use as required.

Makes 150 ml (¼ pt)

GARLIC ALMOND AND PINE NUT SALAD DRESSING

A textured mayonnaise with a very special flavour, this is somewhat garlicky so if you are not keen on garlic, cut down the quantity but do not omit it completely. This mayonnaise will keep in a covered container in the refrigerator for 3 or 4 weeks.

30 ml (2 tbsp) pine nuts   METAL BLADE
1 clove garlic, peeled
50 g (2 oz) ground almonds

1 size-2 egg
1 egg yolk
2.5 ml (½ tsp) salt
1.25 ml (¼ tsp) white pepper
15 to 30 ml (1 to 2 tbsp) fresh lemon juice
150 ml (¼ pt) olive oil (lukewarm)

Switch on the machine and while the motor is running add the pine nuts through the feed tube, processing until they are finely chopped. Without switching off add the garlic and when this is chopped, add the ground almonds, egg, egg yolk and seasoning. Process until fluffy and light in colour. Scrape down the sides of the bowl, add the lemon juice and process to mix. Switch on the motor and while the machine is running, add the oil through the feed tube in a steady trickle. Process continuously until the mixture thickens. Serve with salads, fish, vegetables and poultry.

Makes about 450 ml (¾ pt)

GINGERBREAD MEN

Gingerbread-men cutters can be obtained at most hardware shops although you can of course use an ordinary biscuit cutter.

225 g (8 oz) self-raising flour   METAL BLADE
15 ml (1 tbsp) ground ginger
100 g (4 oz) caster sugar
100 g (4 oz) softened butter or soft margarine
1 size-4 egg

For the topping:
175 g (6 oz) icing sugar, sifted

Put the flour, ginger and sugar into the processor bowl and add the butter or margarine. Process until the mixture resembles breadcrumbs. While the machine is still running add the egg through the feed tube and process to a stiff paste. Turn the mixture on to a lightly floured work surface and roll to a 3 mm (⅛ in) thickness. Cut out the biscuits with the cutter and, using a fish slice, lift the gingerbread men carefully on to greased or non-stick-paper-lined baking sheets. Bake in a fairly hot oven, 200 °C (400°F) Gas Mark 6, for 10 to 15 minutes or until the biscuits are golden brown. Transfer carefully to a cooling wire and leave until cold. (Bake the raw ginger-bread trimmings, leave them to cool, then finally chop in the processor to use as a garnish for custards or puddings.)

Either in a small bowl or in the food processor mix the icing sugar with sufficient water to form a very thick icing. Make a small piping bag from a diagonally folded 20 cm (8 in) square of greaseproof paper and snip the corner from the bottom of the cone. Fill the bag with the icing and pipe eyes, nose and a mouth on each gingerbread man. Store the gingerbread men in an airtight container.

Makes about 16

GREEN VELVET TERRINE

A starter or light supper dish which has a soft delicate texture and a deep green colour. The terrine is easy to prepare and although it can be served as a soft hot pâté, it is best when cold.

450 g (1 lb) fresh spinach leaves,   METAL BLADE
   cooked and drained
175 g (6 oz) veal, cubed
50 g (2 oz) ham
30 ml (2 tbsp) sautéed onion purée (page 194)

15 g (½ oz) butter
100 g (4 oz) fresh breadcrumbs
30 ml (2 tbsp) milk
5 ml (1 tsp) mixed dried herbs
3 size-3 eggs
Salt
Pepper

Put the spinach into the processor bowl and process until puréed. While the machine is running drop the veal and the ham, roughly cut up, through the feed tube and process until finely chopped. Remove the lid, scrape down the sides of the bowl, then add the remaining ingredients, seasoning to taste. Process until the mixture is smooth, scraping down the sides of the bowl twice during processing. Spoon the mixture into a greased loaf tin or Pyrex loaf shape and stand the tin in a baking dish half-filled with hot water. Cover the tin with greased foil and bake in a fairly hot oven, 200°C (400°F) Gas Mark 6, for 1¼ hours. Serve at once from the tin or leave to cool. If serving cold put a weight on top of the foil cover (a similarly sized tin filled with cold water is suitable), then chill for 24 hours. Unmould before slicing.

Serves 6 to 8

HAPPY PUDDING

I would describe this as a family dessert. Nowadays dinner guests often prefer a nice hot home-made pudding to a cold dessert from the trolley.

100 g (4 oz) butter or margarine   **METAL BLADE**
100 g (4 oz) dark soft brown sugar
2 size-2 eggs
2.5 ml (½ tsp) vanilla essence

30 ml (2 tbsp) rum
40 g (1½ oz) dessicated coconut
1 × 398 g (14 oz) can pineapple pieces, drained
100 g (4 oz) self-raising flour
25 g (1 oz) cornflour

Cut the butter or margarine into five or six pieces and place in the processor bowl with the sugar. Process until soft and creamy. While the motor is still running add the eggs through the feed tube one at a time, followed by the vanilla essence and rum. Remove the lid and add half the coconut, the pineapple pieces and half the flour and cornflour. Pulse until all the flour is incorporated. Remove the lid once more and add the remaining flour and cornflour and pulse two or three times until the flour is just mixed in. Turn the mixture into a greased 900 ml (1½ pt) pie dish or round casserole, sprinkle the remaining desiccated coconut on top of the mixture and bake in a moderate oven 180°C (350°F) Gas Mark 4, for 40 to 50 minutes or until the top is golden brown. Serve hot straight from the dish with egg custard, cornflour custard or freshly whipped cream.

Serves 4

HAZELNUT COFFEE CAKE

The coffee in the title means that the cake should be eaten with a cup of coffee. The coffee in the cake is to give slight nuance only. If you wish, you can add an extra 5 ml (1 tsp) of coffee powder or granules.

75 g (3 oz) shelled hazelnuts   METAL BLADE
100 g (4 oz) softened butter or soft margarine
150 g (5 oz) soft brown sugar
2 size-2 eggs

10 ml (2 tsp) instant coffee powder or granules
90 ml (6 tbsp) milk
2.5 ml (½ tsp) bicarbonate of soda
5 ml (1 tsp) baking powder
225 g (8 oz) self-raising flour

For the topping:
30 ml (2 tbsp) grated dessert chocolate

Switch on the machine and put the hazelnuts into the feed
tube while the motor is running. Switch off when the
hazelnuts are finely chopped (the fragments should be tiny
but the nuts should not be pulverized). Remove the lid
and place the butter, sugar, eggs, coffee powder, milk,
bicarbonate of soda and baking powder in the processor
bowl. Process until the mixture is well blended. Remove
the lid, add half the flour to the processor bowl and pulse
five or six times. Remove the lid, add the remaining flour
and pulse only until no further flour particles are visible.

Spoon the mixture into an 18 cm (7 in) deep round cake
tin which has been thoroughly greased and base-lined with
non-stick paper. Smooth the top of the cake mixture with
a palette knife and bake in a very moderate oven, 160°C
(325°F) Gas Mark 3, for 45 to 55 minutes or until the cake
is resilient to the touch. Turn the cake out of the tin,
remove the lining paper and stand the cake on a wire rack.
While the cake is still hot sprinkle the top with the grated
chocolate.

Serves 8 to 10

HOME FARM SHEET CAKE

The apple in this recipe keeps the cake very moist,
enhancing its keeping qualities, but the flavour of the
apple is not apparent in the finished cake. The mixture

reaches to the top of the spindle on smaller food processors. It is however sticky and unlikely to overflow.

225 to 250 g (8 to 9 oz) cooking apples, peeled, cored and quartered	GRATING DISC METAL BLADE

150 g (5 oz) soft margarine
30 ml (2 tbsp) milk
2 size-3 eggs
225 g (8 oz) soft brown sugar
2.5 ml (½ tsp) salt
5 ml (1 tsp) bicarbonate of soda
5 ml (1 tsp) baking powder
2.5 ml (½ tsp) grated nutmeg
225 g (8 oz) plain flour, sifted

Grease a 34 × 24 cm (13 × 9 in) Swiss roll tin and line the base with non-stick or greaseproof paper. If using greaseproof paper grease both its surfaces. Attach the grating disc, put the apple quarters through the feed tube and process, using gentle pressure on the pusher. Leaving the apple in the bowl, remove the grating disc and attach the metal blade, making sure that it is well secured. Place all the remaining ingredients except the flour in the processor bowl and process until the mixture is creamy. (It may look curdled but this is not important.) Remove the lid and distribute half the flour over the surface of the mixture. Pulse once or twice. Add the remaining flour and pulse to fold in, in the same way. Spread the cake mixture evenly into the prepared tin, smoothing the surface with a palette knife. Bake in a moderate oven, 180°C (350°F) Gas Mark 4, for 40 to 45 minutes or until the top of the cake is shiny, golden and resilient to the touch. Turn the cake out on to a wire rack, leave to cool, then cut into fingers. I find four cuts lengthwise and seven cuts widthways produce the best shapes.

Makes 28 pieces

HOME-MADE PASTA

Use this pasta for ravioli, manicotti, canelloni or noodles.
It is easy to make and easy to roll out but remember to roll
very thinly.

275 g (10 oz) plain flour   METAL BLADE
5 ml (1 tsp) salt
15 g (½ oz) soft margarine
1 size-2 egg
30 to 60 ml (2 to 4 tbsp) lukewarm water

Put the flour, salt, margarine and egg into the processor
bowl. Switch on the machine and pour in 2 tablespoons of
the water through the feed tube. Process for 10 seconds,
then remove the lid and feel the dough (take care not to
touch the metal blade). The dough should be soft but
manageable. If not, switch on again and add the remaining water. Turn the dough on to a lightly floured work
surface and use as required.

Enough for 4 to 6 servings

HONEY AND BANANA FRUIT CURD

Serve this unusual spread on hot buttered toast or freshly
cooked dropped scones, or leave it until it is absolutely
cold and use as a cake filling. The curd can be cooked
equally well in the microwave oven – suggested timing 4 to
5 minutes on full power.

Juice and grated rind of 2 small lemons   METAL BLADE
4 medium unblemished bananas
100 g (4 oz) clear honey
50 g (2 oz) unsalted butter at room temperature
2 size-2 eggs, threads removed

Put the lemon juice and rind into the processor bowl, switch on the machine and add the peeled bananas through the feed tube. Process until the bananas are puréed. Scrape down the sides of the bowl and add the honey, butter and eggs. Process until thoroughly blended, then put the mixture into the top half of a double saucepan or in a bowl over a pan one-third filled with hot water and set over medium heat. Cook for 10 to 15 minutes, stirring continuously, until the curd thickens sufficiently to coat the back of a spoon.

The curd will keep for 1 to 2 weeks in the refrigerator and if you decide to do this, pot in the usual way in sterilized jars.

Enough for two 450 g (1 lb) jars

HONIGEN FRUIT LOAF

Although delicious eaten fresh, the loaf will slice more easily if stored for 12 hours before cutting.

2 large bananas   METAL BLADE
200 g (7 oz) self-raising flour
1.25 ml (¼ tsp) bicarbonate of soda
2.5 ml (½ tsp) salt
100 g (4 oz) light soft brown sugar
75 g (3 oz) soft margarine or softened butter
2 size-2 eggs
30 ml (2 tbsp) clear honey
100 g (4 oz) sultanas
75 g (3 oz) raisins
25 g (1 oz) currants

For brushing:
30 ml (2 tbsp) clear honey

Peel the bananas, break each into three or four pieces and put into the processor bowl. Process until mashed. Remove the lid and add the flour, bicarbonate of soda, salt, sugar, margarine or butter, eggs and honey and process until smooth, about 30 seconds. Remove the lid, add the fruits and process briefly to fold them in.

Pour the mixture into a well-greased 20.5 × 10 × 7.5 cm (8 × 4 × 3 in) loaf tin and bake in a moderate oven, 180°C (350°F) Gas Mark 4, for 1¼ to 1½ hours until well risen and resilient to the touch. Have a look at the loaf after about 45 minutes and if it seems to be browning too much, cover the top with a piece of foil.

Turn out the cooked bread on to a wire rack, turn the right way up and brush the top with honey. If you do this while the bread is hot the honey will melt and spread easily. Serve thickly buttered or with jam and cream.

Makes 1 × 450 g (1 lb) loaf

ICED CUCUMBER SOUP

To give added colour, 2 or 3 drops of green food colouring may be mixed in when puréeing.

2 cucumbers, peeled and cut   METAL BLADE
   into chunks
600 ml (1 pt) well-flavoured chicken stock
400 ml (⅔ pt) milk
Salt
Pepper
90 ml (6 tbsp) soured cream

For garnish:
30 ml (2 tbsp) freshly chopped chives (page 57)

Switch on the machine and while the motor is running drop the cucumber pieces through the feed tube. Process to a purée. Add 150 ml (¼ pt) of the chicken stock and process once more to ensure that the mixture is completely smooth. Scrape down the sides of the bowl once during processing.

Pour the purée into a large saucepan and add the remaining stock. Bring to the boil and simmer without covering for 10 to 15 minutes or until the mixture becomes thicker. Stir in the milk and bring back to the boil, then remove from the heat and leave to cool. Season to taste with salt and pepper. Beat in the soured cream and adjust the seasoning if necessary. Chill for 4 hours on the upper shelf of the refrigerator, then pour into a tureen or individual serving bowls and garnish with freshly chopped chives at the moment of serving.

Serves 6 to 7

IRRESISTIBLE CRISPS

Some people like to make these round, some prefer to use a fancy cutter and others find it easiest to cut into domino shapes.

150 g (5 oz) plain flour	METAL BLADE
25 g (1 oz) cornflour	
50 g (2 oz) caster sugar	
100 g (4 oz) butter	

For dredging:
Granulated sugar

Put the flour, cornflour and sugar into the processor bowl, cut the butter into eight pieces and arrange in a circle on top. Put the pusher into the feed tube to prevent particles of the mixture from jumping out and process until the mixture leaves the sides of the processor bowl. Turn out on to a clean surface and gently shape into a soft ball with the hands. Wrap the dough in clingfilm, put into a polythene bag and chill for 45 minutes to firm the dough.

Divide the dough in half and roll out each piece to the thickness of a 5p piece on a well-floured work surface. Cut into rounds with a 4 cm (1½ in) cutter. Gather the trimmings together, knead lightly and repeat the process. Sprinkle the biscuits with granulated sugar, then gently lift them on to an ungreased baking sheet and bake in a very moderate oven, 160°C (325°F) Gas Mark 3, for 9 to 12 minutes or until the biscuits have a dry appearance – they should not colour very much. Transfer the biscuits carefully on to a wire rack using a fish slice and leave until cold. Store in an airtight container.

Makes 24 to 30 depending on the shape and size

JOGGER'S LIQUID BREAKFAST

An energy-packed breakfast light enough to drink before your morning run.

Juice of 4 large oranges   METAL BLADE
15 ml (1 tbsp) fresh lemon juice
1 size-2 egg

Combine all the ingredients in the processor bowl. Insert the pusher in the feed tube and process until the drink is well blended. Strain into a jug or individual glasses – a tea strainer comes in useful for this.

Serves 2

LEMON BRANDY BUTTER

The lemon juice and rind adds a piquancy to the brandy butter, so reducing the rich flavour. If you have been using lemons in other recipes, save the shells and serve the butter in them. It is particularly pretty if the lemons are halved horizontally. Serve with Christmas, suet or steamed sponge puddings.

175 g (6 oz) unsalted butter   METAL BLADE
225 g (8 oz) icing sugar, sieved
30 ml (2 tbsp) brandy
15 ml (1 tbsp) lemon juice
5 ml (1 tsp) grated lemon rind

Cut the butter into eight to ten pieces and arrange in the processor bowl, adding the icing sugar. Insert the pusher in the feed tube and process until the mixture is light and fluffy. Scrape down the sides of the bowl. Add the brandy, lemon juice and rind. Process until well mixed, then pile into a serving dish or lemon shells. Chill in the refrigerator for at least 1 hour before serving.

Serves 8

LIVER PÂTÉ AND EGG DIP

To make an instant dip for a cocktail party use any smooth pâté bought from the local grocers or delicatessen

225 g (8 oz) smooth liver pâté   METAL BLADE
90 ml (6 tbsp) single cream
10 ml (2 tsp) brandy
Salt
Freshly ground black pepper
2 hard-boiled eggs

Put the pâté, cream and brandy into the processor bowl and process until smooth. Taste and adjust the seasoning, scrape down the sides of the bowl and process for 5 to 10 seconds. Remove the lid, add the eggs and pulse until they are finely chopped. Small pieces of chopped egg should still be visible in the pâté. Spoon the dip into the dish and serve with fingers of fresh toast or gri sticks.

Makes about 300 ml (½ pt); serves 6 to 8

LOSELEY OMELETTE

I often buy a large rather than a small carton of yoghurt thinking that I am going to save money and then find that we only eat about half the carton. Then a few days later when we think about having some more we find that it has become fermented. Use up natural yoghurt in this lovely light omelette.

12 chives, washed and well dried   METAL BLADE
6 parsley sprigs
6 eggs
90 ml (6 tbsp) natural yoghurt
Salt
Pepper

For frying:
About 40 g (1½ oz) butter or margarine

Switch on the machine and while the motor is running add the chives and parsley. Process until they are well chopped. Remove the lid, add the eggs and yoghurt and season lightly with salt and pepper, then pulse five or six times until the yoghurt is well incorporated.

Put the butter in a large frying pan and melt over gentle heat. As soon as the butter has melted raise the heat and when it starts to foam, pour in the egg mixture. When the eggs begin to set on the bottom, run a spatula round the edge and tilt the pan so that the liquid egg mixture runs underneath. Continue cooking until the top of the omelette is just set. Using a palette knife slide the omelette on to a hot dish and fold in half. Serve hot.

Serves 3

MARINATED CUCUMBER

When shopping, choose a cucumber that is on the narrow side and then it will fit more easily into the feed tube of your processor.

30 ml (2 tbsp) salad oil　　　　　SLICING DISC
15 ml (1 tbsp) white wine vinegar
15 ml (1 tbsp) dried dill weed
2.5 ml (½ tsp) salt
1 large firm cucumber

Combine the oil, vinegar, dill weed and salt in a wooden salad bowl. Peel the cucumber and remove a slice from the thicker end. Attach the slicing disc and place the cucumber flat end down into the feed tube. Switch on the machine and, holding the top end of the cucumber, process until this end reaches the top of the feed tube. Switch off, insert the pusher and apply gentle pressure while slicing the remainder of the cucumber. Spoon the cucumber slices into the salad dressing and toss so that all the slices are coated. Cover and chill in the refrigerator for 3 to 4 hours before serving.

Serves 6 to 8

MARMALADE CAKES

It is preferable to bake these cakes in paper cases as they sometimes tend to stick. To ensure even rounded shapes, stand the paper cases in individual bun tins.

50 g (2 oz) soft margarine or   METAL BLADE
   softened butter
50 g (2 oz) light soft brown sugar
75 g (3 oz) self-raising flour
2.5 ml (½ tsp) baking powder
2 size-2 eggs
15 ml (1 tbsp) marmalade
30 ml (2 tbsp) orange juice (fresh or canned)

For the filling:
2 to 3 tbsp orange marmalade

Put all the cake ingredients into the processor bowl and process for 20 seconds or until well blended. Do not put the pusher in the feed tube while mixing. Place 12 paper cases into a 12-hole bun tin and half fill each with the cake mixture. Bake on the middle shelf of a moderate oven, 180°C (350°F) Gas Mark 4 for 20 to 25 minutes or until the cakes are well risen and golden. Cool on a wire rack.

When the cakes are cold carefully remove the centres with an apple corer but do not cut through the bottom of the cakes. Fill the holes with marmalade and replace the little plugs of cake, pressing them down lightly.

Makes 12

MAYONNAISE

For perfect mayonnaise all the ingredients should be at the same temperature and I find that room temperature is best when none of the ingredients feels cold to the touch. One of the problems of making mayonnaise in the food processor is that the ingredients become warmer during mixing and by the time half the oil is added, there is a considerable difference between the temperature in the bowl and that of the oil yet to be added and it is at this point that curdling takes place. Follow the instructions carefully and your results will be foolproof. Don't try to double the quantity but rather make up a second batch which can then be mixed in with the first.

1 size-2 egg plus 1 yolk   METAL BLADE
1.25 ml (¼ tsp) dry mustard powder
1.25 ml (¼ tsp) salt
0.625 ml (⅛ tsp) ground white pepper
300 ml (½ pt) good quality vegetable oil
10 ml (2 tbsp) white wine vinegar

Switch on the machine and while the motor is running add the eggs, mustard, salt and pepper through the feed tube. Process until the mixture is pale and creamy. Put the oil into a measuring jug. Switch on the machine and while the motor is running balance the lip of the jug against the rim of the feed tube and aim the oil in a thin steady stream on to the revolving blade. When the mayonnaise is thick, add the vinegar and process briefly just to mix evenly. If the mixture is too thick it may then be thinned down with a little more vinegar or lemon juice.

Store the mayonnaise in a screw-topped jar or tightly covered plastic box in a very cool place or on the bottom shelf of the refrigerator. It will keep for about 3 weeks.

Makes 300 ml (½ pt)

MEAT LOAF

Sometimes more expensive cuts of meat are more economical because there is less waste. For example, 450 g (1 lb) topside could have barely an ounce of fat whereas chuck steak requires much more trimming. The weight given in this recipe is for trimmed meat. If the maximum recommended quantity of meat which can be processed at one time is less than 450 g (1 lb), chop the meat in batches before starting on the recipe.

2 slices bread, crusts removed	METAL BLADE

1 medium onion, peeled and halved
450 g (1 lb) lean beef, cubed
1 × 397 g (14 oz) can tomatoes, drained (reserve juice
   to make sauce)
1 egg
10 ml (2 tsp) salt
2.5 ml (½ tsp) black pepper
10 ml (2 tsp) dried dill weed
Few drops Worcestershire sauce

Switch on the machine and while the motor is running add the bread torn into pieces. As soon as the bread is crumbed add the onion and when this is finely chopped, add the beef through the feed tube a few pieces at a time. Remove the lid and put the tomatoes, egg, salt, pepper, dill weed and Worcestershire sauce into the processor bowl. Insert the pusher in the feed tube and process only until lumps form. Put the meat mixture into a greased round casserole or Pyrex 1.4 litre (2½ pt) loaf shape. Smooth the top with a palette knife and bake in a moderate oven, 180°C (350°F) Gas Mark 4, for 40 to 50 minutes.

Serves 4 to 5

MUSHROOM DUXELLES

A classic mushroom paste which can be used as a sandwich filling, a stuffing in combination with breadcrumbs, a filling for pancakes or simply to flavour soups and sauces.

> 5 to 6 sprigs fresh parsley   METAL BLADE
> 2 shallots, peeled
> 450 g (1 lb) button mushrooms, wiped
> 50 g (2 oz) butter
> Salt
> Pepper

Switch on the machine and while the motor is running add the parsley followed by the shallots and finally the mushrooms and process until finely chopped. Spoon the mixture into a pan and add the butter. Add a little salt and pepper and cook, stirring constantly, over gentle heat until the juices have evaporated leaving a dark coloured paste. Use as required. The mixture may be frozen in covered containers for future use.

Makes 175 g (6 oz)

NON-ALCOHOLIC PARTY PUNCH

> 398 g (14 oz) can red cherries   METAL BLADE
> 1 dessert apple
> 1.25 ml (¼ tsp) ground mace
> 1.25 ml (¼ tsp) ground ginger
> 300 ml (½ pt) concentrated orange juice
> 1 litre (1¾ pt) soda water
> Ice cubes

Drain the cherries and reserve the juice. Stone the cherries. Peel, core and quarter the apple. Put the cherries and apple together with the spices in the processor bowl and process until the fruit is chopped. While the machine is still running add the orange juice through the feed tube, then quickly insert the pusher. Pour the mixture into a jug or bowl, chill in the refrigerator until required, then stir in the soda water and ice cubes.

Serves 8 to 10

PINEAPPLE CAKE

This is a moist plain cake which includes a lot of pineapple to give it a special fruity flavour.

175 g (6 oz) butter, room temperature   METAL BLADE
175 g (6 oz) soft dark brown sugar
100 g (4 oz) self-raising flour
100 g (4 oz) wholemeal flour
10 ml (2 tsp) baking powder
3 size-3 eggs
10 ml (2 tsp) Kirsch
1 × 439 g (15½ oz) can unsweetened pineapple
    pieces, drained (reserve the juice for drinking)

Put the butter, sugar, flours, baking powder, eggs and Kirsch into the processor bowl and, without inserting the pusher into the tube, process for 15 seconds until the mixture is smooth. Add the drained pineapple pieces and process only sufficiently to mix in the pineapple without chopping it completely. Pour the mixture into a greased and base-lined round deep 18 cm (7 in) cake tin and bake in a very moderate oven, 160°C (325°F) Gas Mark 3, for 1¼ to 1½ hours or until the cake is golden on top and resilient to the touch. Turn out on to a wire rack, peel away the paper and serve the cake upside-down.

Serves 8 to 10

PIQUANT TOMATO SALAD

You can use dried herbs in this salad because the herbs are cooked and then left to soak for a long time before serving which causes them to soften and swell.

1 small onion, peeled   METAL BLADE
450 g (1 lb) very small firm tomatoes   SLICING DISC.
45 ml (3 tbsp) red wine vinegar
10 ml (2 tsp) sugar
1.25 ml (¼ tsp) ground black pepper
1.25 ml (¼ tsp) salt
10 ml (2 tsp) dried chives
10 ml (2 tsp) dried parsley

Attach the metal blade and put the onion, cut in half, into the processor bowl and process until chopped but not puréed. Remove the blade and, leaving the onion in the processor bowl, attach the slicing disc. Before switching on the machine stack two or three tomatoes into the feed tube. Process into slices, then switch the machine off. Repeat until all the tomatoes are sliced.

Arrange the tomatoes and onions in a serving dish. Mix together the vinegar, sugar, pepper, salt and herbs in a small saucepan and bring to the boil, stirring continuously. Pour over the tomatoes. Leave until cool, then cover and store in the refrigerator for 6 to 8 hours before serving. Serve as an accompaniment to cold meat or poultry or as a starter.

Serves 6 to 8

PIZZA SCONE BASE

A scone base is suitable for all quick pizzas. If you have a freezer you can prepare a large quantity of flour/margarine crumbs which you can freeze for future use. You will need 90 to 100 ml (6 to 7 tbsp) water for every 275 g (10 oz) of dry mix. All you need to do then is combine the water and crumbs in the food processor.

225 g (8 oz) self-raising flour	METAL BLADE
Pinch salt	
Shake white pepper	
50 g (2 oz) margarine or butter	
90 to 100 ml (6 to 7 tbsp) lukewarm water	

Put the flour, salt, pepper and margarine, cut into four pieces, into the bowl and process to fine crumbs. Switch on the machine and while the motor is running add sufficient water through the feed tube to mix to a soft dough, which will begin to gather round the metal blade in a ball.

Turn the dough out on to a floured work surface and roll out to a 28 cm (11 in) circle. Carefully lift this on to a lightly floured baking tray and fold a 2 cm (1 in) border back and under to form a thick rim all round. Spread your chosen topping over the scone base, leaving the rim plain, then brush the uncovered edges with vegetable oil. Bake in a hot oven, 220°C (425°F) Gas Mark 7, for 20 to 30 minutes, depending upon the filling.

Makes one medium pizza

PLAIN DUMPLINGS

The secret of a light dumpling is in the handling, so do not over-mix once you have added the water. Add the dumplings to the bubbling stew and simmer for 20 minutes before serving.

100 g (4 oz) plain flour   METAL BLADE
15 ml (1 tbsp) baking powder
1.25 ml (¼ tsp) salt
50 g (2 oz) shredded suet or margarine
Approx. 60 ml (4 tbsp) cold water

Put the flour, baking powder and salt into the bowl and process to mix them together. Remove the lid and add the suet or margarine cut into cubes. Without putting the pusher in the feed tube process until the mixture resembles crumbs. Remove the lid and spoon 3 tablespoons of water over the surface of the crumbs, then pulse two or three times to mix into a soft dough. If the mixture seems to be too firm add one more tablespoon of water and pulse once or twice to mix. Turn the mixture on to a lightly floured work surface and divide into eight pieces. Gently shape into balls and use as required.

Makes 8

PLAIN SCONES

Make these when you need something quick for tea and you have no eggs in the larder.

350 g (12 oz) self-raising flour   METAL BLADE
Pinch salt
125 g (4 oz) soft margarine
75 g (3 oz) caster sugar
6 to 7 tbsp milk

Put the flour, salt, margarine and sugar into the bowl and process until the mixture forms tiny lumps. While the machine is still running add just sufficient milk to form a firm dough which draws away slightly from the sides of the bowl. Turn the dough out on to a floured work surface and using a rolling pin or clenched fist, press the dough down to a 2 cm (¾ in) thickness. Use a 5 cm (2 in) cutter or an upturned glass to cut out the scones. Quickly and with only sufficient kneading to remove the cracks, shape and cut scones from the trimmings. Bake in a fairly hot oven, 200°C (400°F) Gas Mark 6, for 12 to 18 minutes until the scones are well risen and golden brown. Split in half and serve with butter, jam and cream or all three together.

Makes about 15

POTTED CHEESE AND HAM

Made in a jiffy, you can serve this as a pâté or a sandwich filling.

    100 g (4 oz) Cheshire cheese   METAL BLADE
    25 g (1 oz) butter
    25 g (1 oz) lean ham
    15 ml (1 tbsp) brandy

Break up the cheese into about three pieces and place in the processor bowl with the butter, the ham roughly torn and the brandy. Process until very smooth, scraping down the sides of the bowl once or twice. Spoon the mixture into a pretty stoneware jar or dish and refrigerate for 1 hour before serving.

Serves 4

POULETTE SAUCE

A special sauce to serve with poultry, fish, vegetables or eggs. Use fish stock for fish and chicken stock for other dishes.

50 g (2 oz) unsalted butter · · · · · METAL BLADE
300 ml (½ pt) hot stock
30 ml (2 tbsp) double cream
Juice half lemon
1 egg yolk
30 ml (2 tbsp) flour
Salt
Pepper

Switch on the machine and add the ingredients through the feed tube in the order given. Do not over-season at this stage. Pour the mixture into a heavy-based saucepan and stir continuously over the lowest possible heat until the sauce thickens. Cook for 1 or 2 more minutes.

Makes 300 ml (½ pt)

PRAWN DIP

Serve with raw vegetables, crisps, prawn crackers or tiny strips of deep-fried fish.

100 g (4 oz) cooked peeled prawns · · · · · METAL BLADE
150 ml (¼ pt) mayonnaise (page 127)
30 ml (2 tbsp) curry powder
15 ml (1 tbsp) fresh lemon juice

Put all the ingredients into the processor bowl. Process until smooth, scraping down the sides of the bowl once or twice. Spoon the dip into a serving dish, cover and chill for about 1 hour before serving.

Makes about 200 ml (7 fl oz); serves 8 to 10

PRETZEL CHEESE PÂTÉ

This is an attractive way to serve a home-made soft cheese for a party. Although the recipe uses fresh chives, if these are not available you can use frozen chopped chives but don't attempt to chop frozen whole chives in the food processor because they will only become puréed. The pretzels soften after a few hours, so garnish towards serving time.

8 fresh chives, dried in kitchen paper   METAL BLADE
2 cocktail gherkins
225 g (8 oz) curd cheese
100 g (4 oz) butter
Dash Tabasco

For garnish:
Small packet pretzels
5 to 10 ml (1 to 2 tsp) coarsely ground black pepper

Make sure that the bowl, blade and chives are absolutely dry, then switch on the machine and add the chives. As soon as these are chopped and with the motor still running, add the gherkins. Remove the lid, add the cheese, the butter cut into about six pieces and the Tabasco. Process to a smooth paste, scraping down the sides of the bowl once. Remove the cheese mixture from the bowl and shape into a round cake. Break pretzels into lengths the height of the cake and press around the cheese to form a fence. Crumble the remaining pretzels and press on top of the cheese. Sprinkle with the black pepper.

Serves 8

RICOTTA FILLING FOR PASTA

Use this filling for ravioli, canelloni or manicotti. It is enough to fill eight pasta tubes or sixty ravioli squares.

30 ml (2 tbsp) parsley sprigs   METAL BLADE
225 g (8 oz) riccotta cheese
1.25 ml (¼ tsp) salt
1.25 (¼ tsp) pepper
30 ml (2 tbsp) grated Parmesan cheese

Put the parsley sprigs into the processor bowl and process continuously until finely chopped. Remove the lid, add the ricotta, seasonings and Parmesan cheese and process until mixed to a paste. Use at once or transfer to a sealed plastic container and store in the refrigerator for up to 3 days or in the freezer for 1 month.

Enough for 6 portions

RUMBLES

Rumbles are a type of no-cook truffle using cake or biscuit left-overs but the cake must be stale if the recipe is to be successful.

150 g (6 oz) shelled walnuts   METAL BLADE
150 g (6 oz) stale cake or sweet biscuits
100 g (4 oz) icing sugar, sieved
30 ml (2 tbsp) cocoa, sieved
1.25 ml (¼ tsp) ground mixed spice
Pinch ground ginger
30 ml (2 tbsp) golden syrup
60 ml (4 tbsp) rum

For dusting:
Icing sugar

Switch on the machine and while the motor is running add the walnuts and cake or biscuits through the feed tube. Process until the mixture is very finely chopped. Open the lid and add the icing sugar, cocoa, spices, syrup and rum. Insert the pusher in the feed tube and process until the mixture forms a ball. Divide the mixture into about thirty even pieces and with hands dusted with icing sugar shape into balls. Store in an airtight container in the refrigerator, separating the layers with greaseproof paper. If the container is not airtight the sugar coating may begin to dissolve.

Makes 30

SATSUMA MADEIRA CAKE

Half an orange can be substituted for the satsuma.

175 g (6 oz) butter or margarine at   METAL BLADE
   room temperature
175 g (6 oz) caster sugar
225 g (8 oz) plain flour
7.5 ml (1½ tsp) baking powder
3 size-3 eggs
1 satsuma, peeled and segmented

Put the butter (or margarine) and sugar into the processor bowl and process until fluffy. While the motor is still running add through the feed tube one heaped tablespoon of the flour, all the baking powder, then the eggs and the satsuma segments, added one at a time. As soon as the mixture is well blended, remove the lid and distribute half the remaining flour over the surface of the cake mixture.

Replace the lid and pulse three times until no flour particles are visible. Repeat with the remaining flour. Turn the mixture into a greased and fully lined 18 cm (7 in) round cake tin and bake in a very moderate oven, 160°C (325°F) Gas Mark 3, for 1½ to 1¾ hours or until the cake is golden brown and crisp on the outside. The cake rises to an attractive peak in the middle.

Makes about 12 portions

SAUTÉED POTATO SLICES

Very fattening but the children will love them. Some potatoes are waxier than others and I prefer to use Red Skins or Maris Piper rather than King Edwards.

450 g (1 lb) potatoes   SLICING DISC
50 g (2 oz) butter
15 ml (1 tbsp) oil
Salt

Peel the potatoes and cut into pieces that will fit the width of the feed tube. Fill the feed tube with potatoes, flat sides down and process in batches, using medium pressure on the pusher. Tip the sliced potatoes into a colander and run them under a hot tap or put them into a mixing bowl and cover with boiling water. Stir the potatoes during this process to remove surplus starch and to separate the slices. Drain thoroughly and shake the slices in a clean teacloth. Heat the butter and oil in a saucepan or frying pan and when the butter sizzles, add the potato slices in two batches, turning them over during cooking. When they are crisp and brown around the edges, remove from the pan and drain on kitchen paper. Sprinkle with salt just before serving.

Serves 3 as a vegetable or 4 as a garnish

SAVOURY FISH BUTTER

To give additional flavour, top fish with a pat of savoury butter before steaming, grilling or baking.

100 g (4 oz) butter	METAL BLADE
2.5 ml (½ tsp) dried basil	
2.5 ml (½ tsp) dried marjoram	
2.5 ml (½ tsp) dried savory	
2.5 ml (½ tsp) freshly ground black pepper	
2.5 ml (½ tsp) salt	
Juice of half lemon	

Cut the butter into cubes and place in a circle in the processor bowl. Add all the other ingredients. Process until all the ingredients are well mixed in, scraping down the sides of the bowl once. If you find that some of the lemon juice is running free, remove the metal blade and mix in with a spoon.

Place the savoury butter in a covered pot and store in the refrigerator for up to 2 weeks. Alternatively shape the butter into a sausage, roll up in greaseproof paper and twist the ends Christmas cracker fashion and chill. Open the package, slice into butter pats and freeze in a single layer or layers separated by greaseproof paper in a covered container for up to 3 months.

Makes about 16 pats

SCOTCH SHORTBREAD

To prevent the shortbread from spreading during baking cook in a flan ring. Halve the recipe when using a small-capacity food-processor bowl.

200 g (8 oz) plain flour   METAL BLADE
200 g (8 oz) rice flour
50 g (2 oz) caster sugar
100 g (4 oz) unsalted butter

For dusting:
Caster sugar

Put the flours and sugar into the processor bowl and process for 10 seconds. Remove the lid and arrange the butter cut into eight pieces on the dry mixture. Insert the pusher into the feed tube and process to a smooth dough which forms a ball around the blade. Remove the dough from the processor bowl, divide into two and press each half into an 18 cm (7 in) flan ring first placed on a baking tray. Prick the surface thoroughly, then bake the shortbread in a moderately hot oven, 190°C (375°F) Gas Mark 5, for 20 to 25 minutes until golden brown. Remove the flan rings, sprinkle the shortbread with sugar and mark into six or eight wedges.

Makes 12 to 16 pieces

SHORTCRUST PASTRY

150 g (6 oz) plain flour   METAL BLADE
Pinch salt
75 g (3 oz) hard margarine or butter
Ice-cold water

Put the flour and the salt in the processor bowl and add the margarine cut into four or five pieces. Insert the pusher in the feed tube and process until the mixture resembles breadcrumbs. While the motor is still running pour in 30 to 37 ml (2 to 2½ tbsp) cold water through the feed tube and process to a smooth firm dough which forms a ball around the blade. Wrap the dough in polythene and refrigerate for at least 30 minutes before using.

Makes enough to line one 18 or 20.5 cm (7 or 8 in) flan ring

SHRIMP CAKES

Truly Chinese, very expensive and worth it.

1 × 1 cm (½ in) slice ginger root   **METAL BLADE**
1 white part spring onion
550 g (1¼ lb) cooked shelled shrimps or small prawns
6 canned water chestnuts, drained
1 size-3 egg
5 ml (1 tsp) salt
2.5 ml (½ tsp) pepper
5 ml (1 tsp) cornflour
15 ml (1 tbsp) dry white wine or sherry
5 ml (1 tsp) vegetable oil

For frying:
Oil

Switch on the machine and while the motor is running add the ginger and the spring onion. When these are chopped finely and with the motor still running, add the shrimps, followed by the water chestnuts, through the feed tube and process until pulped. Scrape down the sides of the processor bowl. Switch on again and add the egg, seasonings and cornflour and lastly the wine and oil. Process until all the ingredients are well blended. Heat 1 cm (½ in) oil in a frying pan and gently fry the soft mixture in spoonfuls, turning the patties over half-way through the cooking. Serve as an appetizer, starter or a light supper dish with salad.

Makes 12 to 16

SIMPLE WHITE SAUCE

Use a neutral-flavoured good-quality vegetable oil such as sunflower oil. Sauces made with oil have no pronounced flavour, so that you can add flavouring or colouring to suit yourself. Grated cheese, chopped anchovies, chopped hard-boiled egg and freshly chopped herbs are a few suggestions for savoury sauces. For sweet sauces omit the salt and pepper and add honey, syrup, grated chocolate or puréed fruit. The proportions given are for a coating sauce. Add more or less liquid to achieve a thinner or thicker consistency.

60 ml (4 tbsp) plain flour   METAL BLADE
30 ml (2 tbsp) vegetable oil
300 ml (½ pt) milk
Salt
Pepper
Chosen ingredients

Put all the ingredients into the processor bowl and process until the mixture is smooth and lump-free. Pour the sauce into a pan and cook over medium heat, stirring continuously with a wooden spoon until the sauce thickens. Switch off the heat and continue stirring for a further 1 to 2 minutes. Stir in the flavourings.

Makes 300 ml (½ pt)

SMOKED TROUT PÂTÉ

Smoked trout has a pinker flesh and a more delicate flavour than smoked mackerel although the latter is cheaper and sometimes easier to obtain. Use whole fish or fillets but do remember to remove not only the heads and skins, but also every single bone. Although the food processor is superb at chopping and blending, bones that are fine and lie flat can sometimes slip through undetected.

2 slices white bread, crusts removed   METAL BLADE
15 to 30 ml (1 to 2 tbsp) milk
Flesh only of two large smoked trout
Juice of 1 medium lemon
30 ml (2 tbsp) horseradish sauce
50 g (2 oz) unflavoured cottage cheese
150 ml (¼ pt) soured cream
75 g (3 oz) butter, softened
Salt
Pepper

For garnish:
Lemon slices
Sliced olives
Paprika

Switch on the machine and while the motor is running add the bread, torn into pieces, through the feed tube. As soon as the bread is crumbed pour in the milk spoon by spoon, adding only sufficient to moisten, but not soak, the breadcrumbs. Remove the lid and place all the other ingredients except the salt and pepper in the processor bowl. Process until the mixture is smooth, scraping down the sides of the bowl once. Taste, season if necessary and process briefly. Spoon the pâté into individual ramekins or a larger pâté dish and garnish with lemon slices, sliced olives and a shake of paprika.

Serves 6

SUNSET CHERRY LOGS

These are a cross between a biscuit and a cake and harden as they cool. Cut them whilst warm.

40 g (1½ oz) shelled almonds   METAL BLADE
8 glacé cherries
25 g (1 oz) cornflour
2.5 ml (½ tsp) almond essence
175 g (6 oz) plain flour
50 g (2 oz) caster sugar
75 g (3 oz) butter

Put the almonds into the processor bowl and process until finely chopped. Remove half the chopped almonds and set aside. Add the cherries and the cornflour to the bowl, then process until chopped into pea-sized pieces, scraping down the sides of the bowl once. Remove the lid and put the almond essence, flour, sugar and butter (cut into about six pieces) into the processor bowl and process until the mixture forms a crumbly sticky dough. Press the dough into a 20.5 cm (8 in) square tin, using the back of a spoon. Sprinkle the reserved almonds over the entire surface, then press in thoroughly. Bake the cake in a very moderate oven, 160°C (325°F) Gas Mark 3, for 30 to 40 minutes or until the mixture has risen and is puffy on top. Test with a skewer, which should come out clean. Cut into fingers and leave in the tin until cool.

Makes 12

SWEET PICKLE AND OLIVE MINCED BEEF LOAF

Pickle is often thought of as just a component part of the Ploughman's lunch but it is also a most interesting ingredient to mix into other dishes. I've used it here in conjunction with olives to make a perfectly ordinary minced dish just a little bit different. The texture is coarse and crumbly and is popular with our family and friends.

With some machines the recommended maximum quantity for chopping meat is 225 g (8 oz). For these models, therefore, it will be necessary to chop the meat in this recipe in two batches, then transfer it all to a mixing bowl. Process the remaining ingredients, add to the meat and mix by hand.

450 g (1 lb) lean beef cut into cubes   METAL BLADE
1 small onion, peeled
50 g (2 oz) stuffed green olives
40 g (1½ oz) porridge oats
5 ml (1 tsp) salt
1.25 ml (¼ tsp) pepper
1.25 ml (¼ tsp) ground nutmeg
30 ml (2 tbsp) tomato ketchup
45 ml (3 tbsp) sweet pickle
1 egg

Put the meat into the processor bowl and process until coarsely chopped. While the motor is still running add the onion, followed by the olives; as soon as the olives are chopped, switch off the machine. Remove the lid, add the remaining ingredients and process until mixed. Put the mixture into a 750 ml (1¼ pt) loaf tin and smooth the top but do not press down. Bake in a moderate oven, 180°C (350°F) Gas Mark 4, for 40 minutes when the top of the loaf will be brown and crusty and the inside just cooked. Turn out carefully, taking care that the meat loaf does not crumble.

Serves 6

TARAMASALATA

Taramasalata consists basically of bread, cod's roe and oil and there are numerous recipes which can be adapted for the food processor. This one will appeal to people who dislike onions but not to those who dislike garlic. Use the basic proportions and vary the flavourings to please yourself.

> 2 slices white bread, crusts removed　　METAL BLADE
> Few tablespoons milk
> 225 g (8 oz) fresh smoked cod's roe *or* 1 × 175 g (6 oz) jar smoked cod's roe
> ½ clove peeled garlic, lightly crushed with a table knife
> 90 ml (6 tbsp) olive oil
> Juice of ½ lemon
> 1.25 ml (¼ tsp) freshly ground pepper
>
> *To garnish:*
> Olives
> Lemon butterflies

Tear up the bread and put the pieces in the processor bowl. Spoon a little milk over the top, then as soon as this has been absorbed, add more milk until the bread is soaked but no liquid is running free. (If you add too much by mistake you can easily spoon out the surplus.) Place the remaining ingredients in the processor bowl and process until the mixture is light and smooth, scraping down the sides of the bowl once or twice. Spoon the pâté into a serving dish and garnish with whole olives or lemon butterflies.

Serves 6

TARRAGON VINAIGRETTE

A delicious variation on the French dressing theme.

    10 ml (2 tsp) fresh tarragon leaves
    30 ml (2 tbsp) walnut oil
    120 ml (4 fl oz) corn oil
    45 ml (3 tbsp) fresh lemon juice
    2.5 ml (½ tsp) white pepper
    2.5 ml (½ tsp) salt

Wash and dry the tarragon leaves thoroughly. Switch on the machine and while the motor is running add the leaves through the feed tube. As soon as the tarragon is finely chopped add the remaining ingredients; make sure that the pusher is in position and process until well mixed, scraping down the sides of the bowl once or twice.

Makes 200 ml (7 fl oz)

THATCHED GOOSEBERRY PIE

Use frozen gooseberries if fresh are not obtainable or if you want to save yourself the bother of trimming the fruit. The topping also goes well with either frozen or fresh rhubarb.

    450 g (1 lb) gooseberries, washed   METAL BLADE
        and trimmed
    75 g (3 oz) caster sugar
    50 g (2 oz) plain flour
    100 g (4 oz) porridge oats
    75 g (3 oz) demerara sugar
    100 g (4 oz) butter
    1 Shredded Wheat

Mix the gooseberries and caster sugar together in a large greased pie dish or round casserole. Put the flour, porridge oats, demerara sugar and 75 g (3 oz) of the butter, cut into pieces, into the processor bowl and process until the mixture forms fine crumbs. Spoon this prepared topping over the fruit, pressing it down with a palette knife. Crush the Shredded Wheat in your hands, sprinkle over the topping, then cover with dabs of the remaining butter. Bake in a moderately hot oven, 190°C (375°F) Gas Mark 5, for 35 to 45 minutes or until the topping is crunchy and golden brown.

Serves 6

TOMATO AND HONEY SALAD DRESSING

6 fresh chives, washed and dried   METAL BLADE
30 ml (2 tbsp) tomato juice
30 ml (2 tbsp) fresh lemon juice
60 ml (4 tbsp) walnut oil
15 ml (1 tbsp) clear honey
1 egg yolk, threads removed
Salt
Pepper

Switch on the machine, and while the motor is running add the chives through the feed tube. As soon as the chives are chopped pour in all the remaining ingredients and process until well mixed. Pour over prepared salads just before serving.

Makes 150 ml (¼ pt)

TOMATO SAUCE

This is ideal with all forms of pasta. The thick sauce tends to spatter so it is a good idea to cover the pan partly during cooking.

15 ml (1 tbsp) parsley sprigs   METAL BLADE
2 celery stalks, broken into chunks
1 small onion, peeled and halved
½ clove garlic, peeled
60 ml (4 tbsp) vegetable oil
90 ml (6 tbsp) tomatoe purée
2 × 398 g (14 oz) cans tomatoes
5 ml (1 tsp) dried basil
5 ml (1 tsp) dried oregano
5 ml (1 tsp) salt
5 ml (1 tsp) freshly ground black pepper

Put the parsley sprigs, celery, onion and garlic into the processor bowl and process until puréed. Scrape down the sides of the bowl. Add the oil, tomatoe purée, tomatoes and their juice, herbs and seasonings and process until well blended. Turn the mixture into a heavy-based saucepan, partially cover with the lid and simmer for 20 to 30 minutes, stirring occasionally until the sauce thickens. The sauce can be stored in the refrigerator for 4 or 5 days or in the freezer for up to 2 months.

Makes about 900 ml (1½ pt)

TUNA LOAF

Tuna loaf is very filling. I bake it in the smaller-size foil dishes that I save after buying 'take-aways'. Double the quantity if you wish and use a 450 g (1 lb) loaf tin.

1 small onion, peeled and halved   METAL BLADE
50 g (2 oz) crustless white bread
1 size-2 egg
15 ml (1 tbsp) tomato purée
5 ml (1 tsp) fresh lemon juice
2 × 198 g (7 oz) cans tuna, drained
90 ml (6 tbsp) milk
1.25 ml (¼ tsp) pepper

Switch on the machine and drop the onion through the
feed tube, processing until finely chopped. Without
switching off add the bread torn into pieces. Remove the
processor lid and add the egg, tomato purée, lemon juice,
tuna, milk and pepper and process until the mixture is well
blended, scraping down the sides of the bowl twice. Pack
the mixture firmly into a 15 × 11 cm (6 × 4½ in) greased
foil tin and bake in a moderate oven, 180°C (350°F) Gas
Mark 4, for 35 to 45 minutes or until the loaf is brown on
top. Turn out on to a serving dish and serve hot or cold
with egg and anchovy sauce (page 211).

Serves 4

TUNA PÂTÉ

Use this as a filling for savoury tartlets, as a pâté, or as a
filling for stuffed raw tomatoes; it is equally pleasant as a
sandwich filling.

1 × 198 g (7 oz) can tuna fish in oil   METAL BLADE
100 g (4 oz) black olives, stoned
30 ml (2 tbsp) capers, drained
½ clove garlic
1 egg yolk
Salt
Pepper

For garnish:
Cayenne pepper
Lemon slices

Put the tuna and half its oil, the olives, capers, egg yolk and garlic into the bowl and process until smooth. Taste and add salt and pepper if necessary. Spoon into a dish and sprinkle with Cayenne pepper. Serve decorated with halved lemon slices.

Serves 6 to 8

TURKEY PÂTÉ

Among the 101 ways of using left-over turkey, consider this recipe which requires only 225 g (8 oz) of turkey. Eat within a few hours or store in the freezer where it will keep for 2 or 3 months to be brought out again when you have recovered from the Christmas turkey onslaught.

225 g (8 oz) cooked turkey, roughly   METAL BLADE
   cut up
60 ml (4 tbsp) coating-consistency white sauce
   (page 200)
30 ml (2 tbsp) tomato purée
5 ml (1 tsp) Worcestershire sauce
1 × 78 g (2¾ oz) jar ham paste
60 ml (4 tbsp) double cream

Put the turkey into the processor bowl and process until it is finely chopped. Remove the lid, add the remaining ingredients and process, scraping down the sides of the bowl once, until the paste is smooth and creamy. Spoon into a serving dish and chill for 1 to 2 hours.

Serves 8 to 12

VEGETABLE AND GAMMON SOUP

Here's a soup that you can freeze so that left-overs need not be wasted. The soup takes quite a long time to cook so that if you have a pan big enough you could double the quantity.

225 g (8 oz) trimmed gammon, cubed   METAL BLADE
450 g (1lb) onions, peeled and quartered
2 large leeks, trimmed and washed
1 small turnip, peeled and roughly cut up
2 medium carrots, peeled
450 g (1 lb) potatoes, peeled and cut into small pieces
100 g (4 oz) piece white cabbage
1 × 150 g (6 oz) can baked beans in tomato sauce
Salt
Pepper

Switch on the machine and while the motor is running add the gammon, followed by all the vegetables except the canned beans. You may have to do this in three batches depending on the size of your processor bowl. Put all the prepared ingredients into a large saucepan and add the baked beans in the tomato sauce. Pour in 1.1 litre (2 pt) water, bring to the boil, then reduce the heat and simmer for 1½ to 2 hours until the vegetables and bacon are tender. Season to taste with salt and pepper. Serve with chunks of fresh French bread.

Serves 8 to 10

VEGETABLE CUTLETS

Vegetable cutlets, though suitable for the vegetarian, can also be served as a vegetable with beef, lamb or pork casseroles. Process the recipe in two half quantities if your processor bowl cannot accommodate the total amount.

450 g (1 lb) mixture of cooked   METAL BLADE
   vegetables including onions (a frozen stew pack
   contains a useful mixture)
30 ml (2 tbsp) flour
30 ml (2 tbsp) dried breadcrumbs (page 36)
1 size-4 egg
15 ml (1 tbsp) bottled sauce
1.25 ml (¼ tsp) ground bay leaves
Salt
Pepper

Dried breadcrumbs for coating
Oil for shallow frying

Switch on the machine and spoon the vegetables through the feed tube while the motor is running. Process until they are well packed down in the processor bowl and scrape down the sides of the bowl once. With the motor running add the flour, breadcrumbs, egg, sauce, bay leaf powder, salt and pepper. Process briefly, then taste and adjust the seasoning. Divide the mixture into twelve and shape into patties on a work surface. Sprinkle generously with dried breadcrumbs, pressing them well into the patties on all surfaces. Heat about 1 cm (½ in) oil in a large frying pan and fry the patties on both sides until golden and crisp.

Makes 12

VICTORIA SANDWICH (QUICK MIX)

Very often a Victoria Sandwich has a flat appearance and you may think that this is because you did not cook it properly, but in fact the recommended 100 g (4 oz) each of flour, sugar and fat is insufficient for two 18 cm (7 in) sandwich tins. Increase the quantities and your cake will look well-risen and appetizing.

175 g (6 oz) soft margarine   METAL BLADE
175 g (6 oz) caster sugar
3 size-2 eggs
175 g (6 oz) self-raising flour
5 ml (1 tsp) baking powder

Raspberry jam for filling
Icing sugar for dusting

Put the margarine, sugar, eggs, flour and baking powder into the bowl and without the pusher in position, process for just long enough to mix the ingredients. Switch off as soon as the mixture is creamy. It is important not to overbeat.

Divide the mixture between two 18 cm (7 in) greased and base-lined sandwich tins and smooth the top of the mixture with a palette knife. Bake in a very moderate oven, 160°C (325°F) Gas Mark 3, for 25 to 35 minutes or until the cakes are well risen, golden on top and resilient to the touch. Turn the cakes out on to a wire rack and remove the paper. Leave until cold, then sandwich the cakes with raspberry jam and dredge the top with icing sugar.

Serves 6 to 8

VICTORIA SANDWICH (TRADITIONAL)

The ingredients are practically the same as for the quick-mix cake but the baking powder is omitted. It is essential to incorporate as much air as possible when making this cake in the food processor so therefore the pusher should not be in place during mixing. When adding the flour the cake must be processed in fractions of a second only. Over-processing causes the cake to peak and split. The best way to prevent this it to pulse, i.e. switch the machine on and off. As soon as all the particles of flour are incorporated turn the mixture into the prepared tins. It is better to pour than to spoon, and any smoothing of the surface should be carried out very gently in order to preserve all the air pockets.

175 g (6 oz) butter at room   METAL BLADE
    temperature or soft margarine
175 g (6 oz) caster sugar
3 size-2 eggs
175 g (6 oz) self-raising flour, twice sifted

Jam or icing for filling
Icing sugar for dredging

Cut the butter into four or six pieces and arrange around the inside of the processor bowl. Process until the butter is creamed. Remove the lid, add the sugar and process until the mixture is light and fluffy. While the motor is running add the eggs, one at a time, alternating with one level tablespoon of the sifted flour. As soon as the mixture is creamy remove the lid and sprinkle half the remaining flour over the surface. Pulse two or three times only to incorporate the flour, then repeat with the remaining flour. Pour the mixture, using a plastic spatula to help it along, into two 18 cm (7 in) greased and base-lined sandwich tins and bake in a very moderate oven, 160°C (325°F) Gas Mark 3, for 25 to 35 minutes or until the cakes are well risen and golden brown. Turn out on to a wire rack, remove the paper and leave the cakes until they are cold. Sandwich them together with jam or icing and dredge the top with icing sugar.

Serves 8

WALDORF SALAD

Another variation on the celery, apple and walnut theme. This is a mixture with good keeping qualities and will store in the refrigerator for a few days.

25 g (1 oz) shelled walnuts　　　　METAL BLADE
½ medium red pepper, cored and deseeded
3 celery stalks, trimmed and cut into 2.5 cm (1 in)
　　pieces
2 dessert apples
1.25 ml (¼ tsp) caster sugar
1.25 ml (¼ tsp) salt
1.25 ml (¼ tsp) pepper
15 ml (1 tbsp) fresh lemon juice
15 ml (1 tbsp) olive oil

Put the walnuts and the red pepper, cut into four or six pieces, into the processor bowl and pulse until both are finely chopped. Remove the lid and add the celery, the apples (peeled, cored and quartered), the sugar, salt and pepper. Pour the lemon juice and oil evenly over the surface. Replace the lid and pulse several times until the celery and apples are roughly chopped. Spoon the mixture into a serving dish, cover and store in the refrigerator.

Serves 6

WALNUT AND CELERY SLAW

Provided you grate the walnuts first, you can add the vegetables in any order. I find that if I add them alternately the salad is subsequently easier to mix.

25 g (1 oz) shelled fresh walnuts   GRATING DISC
1 × 175 g (6 oz) piece white cabbage,   (a coarse one
     cut into four pieces that   if you have it)
     will fit the feed tube
1 large carrot, peeled and halved
1 very small onion, peeled
3 celery stalks, trimmed and cut into chunks
30 ml (2 tbsp) soured cream
30 ml (2 tbsp) mayonnaise (page 127)
Salt and pepper to taste

Fill the feed tube with the nuts, insert the pusher and process using light pressure. While the motor is running add the vegetables piece by piece through the feed tube, using firm pressure on the pusher. Remove the lid and the grating disc, add the soured cream and mayonnaise, and mix with a spoon, adding salt and pepper to taste. Spoon into a salad bowl.

Serves 4 to 6

WHIZZ OF FRUIT DESSERT

Use any canned fruit that you like for this recipe and if you prefer a less sweet dessert, choose fruit in natural juice.

1 × 396 g (14 oz) can fruit   METAL BLADE
90 ml (6 tbsp) double cream
150 ml (¼ pt) natural set yoghurt

For decoration:
50 ml (2 tbsp) grated chocolate digestive biscuits

Drain the fruit and put into the processor bowl with the cream and yoghurt. Insert the pusher in the feed tube,

switch on at maximum speed and process until the mixture
is smooth, scraping down the sides of the bowl once.
Divide the purée between three or four stemmed glasses
and chill in the top part of the refrigerator. Do not freeze.
Just before serving sprinkle the dessert with the biscuit
crumbs.

Serves 3

WHOLEWHEAT SCONES

Use stoneground flour and muscovado sugar if you can
obtain them, although you can substitute wholemeal flour
and soft brown sugar but the flavour will not be the same.
The scones are brown and crumbly. I don't glaze them
before baking because I like their rustic appearance.

225 g (8 oz) 100% stoneground plain　　METAL BLADE
   wholewheat flour
15 ml (1 tbsp) baking powder
Pinch salt
75 g (3 oz) butter or margarine
25 g (1 oz) muscovado sugar
1 size-3 egg
60 to 90 ml (4 to 6 tbsp) milk

Put the flour, baking powder, salt, butter cut into about
six pieces, and sugar into the food processor bowl. Process
until the mixture forms large crumbs, then while the
motor is still running, add the egg and 4 tablespoons of the
milk through the feed tube. Remove the lid and inspect
the dough which should be soft but not creamy and show a
tendency to leave the sides of the bowl. Add the extra
milk only if necessary.

Using a plastic spatula turn the dough on to a lightly floured work surface and knead very gently to remove any cracks. Shape into a 15 cm (6 in) square, then cut into three equal lengths. Cut each into three even pieces and space the square scones out on a greased baking sheet. Bake in a hot oven, 220°C (425°F) Gas Mark 7, for 12 to 15 minutes or until the scones are firm to the touch. You cannot tell the amount of 'doneness' by the appearance of these scones as they do not change colour very much. Serve straight from the oven; carefully cut each in half and fill with softened butter.

Makes 9

Step-by-step Recipes

These recipes are designed to save hassle and frayed tempers. They are worked out in sequence so you don't have to wash the processor bowl between processes. When changing the blade or discs remove the processor bowl from the machine before taking out the attachment. It is certainly easier and less hazardous to remove the metal blade before emptying out the processed foods. To maintain efficiency the blade must be sharp. Metal spoons can blunt the edge and plastic spatulas be scratched. You should never remove food with your fingers. After removing the blade or disc use a plastic spatula to scrape food particles from the sides of the bowl, taking a little extra care if the bowl is being used again without a rinse in between.

ALMOND AND LEMON LOAF CAKE

The secret of the soft melt-in-the-mouth texture is due to the use of soft margarine rather than hard margarine or butter. The fat particles can be more easily distributed and the mixture is more quickly blended. The cake has good keeping qualities provided it is stored in an airtight container.

100 g (4 oz) soft margarine   METAL BLADE
100 g (4 oz) caster sugar
75 g (3 oz) self-raising flour
5 ml (1 tsp) baking powder
25 g (1 oz) ground almonds
2 size-2 eggs
5 ml (1 tsp) grated lemon rind

For the icing:
100 g (4 oz) icing sugar
37.5 ml (2½ tbsp) fresh lemon juice

1. Grease and base-line a loaf-shape tin, 20.5 × 10 × 7.5 cm (8 × 4 × 3in).
2. Put all the cake ingredients into the bowl and process for 15 seconds or until just blended. Pour the mixture into the prepared tin and bake in a very moderate oven, 160°C (325°F) Gas Mark 3, for 40 to 45 minutes or until the cake is golden in colour and resilient to the touch.
3. Remove the cake from the tin, take off the paper lining and put the cake on a wire rack over a tray.
4. Wipe the blade and the processor bowl if necessary and put in the icing sugar and lemon juice. Process until the icing is smooth.
5. Spoon the icing over the top of the warm cake, allowing it to run down the sides. Leave until the icing is set before serving.

Cuts into about 12 slices.

ALMOND CAKES

Use up left-over egg whites for this recipe. If your food processor is fitted with a whisk first beat the egg whites and then transfer them to a mixing bowl.

3 size-2 egg whites	**WHISK OPTIONAL**
75 g (3 oz) butter at room	**METAL BLADE**
temperature or soft margarine	
75 g (3 oz) caster sugar	
2.5 ml (½ tsp) almond essence	
100 g (4 oz) self-raising flour	
40 g (1½ oz) ground almonds	

For decoration:
12 blanched almonds
50 g (2 oz) icing sugar

1. Put a paper case into each hole of a 12-hole bun tin and preheat a moderate oven, 180°C (350°F) Gas Mark 4.
2. Whisk the egg whites in a grease-free bowl until stiff.
3. Put the butter and sugar in the processor bowl and add the almond essence. Process until the mixture is light and fluffy. Add the flour and ground almonds and process to mix.
4. Remove the lid, top the mixture with half the beaten egg white and pulse twice only, then remove the lid once more and add the remaining egg white. Pulse only until the egg white is incorporated and the mixture is foamy.
5. Spoon the cake mixture evenly into the paper cases in the tin and bake for 12 to 18 minutes or until the cakes are well risen and resilient to the touch.
6. Remove the cakes from the tin and cool on a wire rack.
7. While the cakes are cooling roughly chop the almonds in the food processor. Remove and set aside.

8. Put the icing sugar into the processor bowl with 7½ ml (1½ tsp) hot water and process to a smooth paste.
9. Spoon a little icing in the centre of each cake and sprinkle with the almonds.

Makes 12

BÉCHAMEL SAUCE

The quantities given produce a sauce the consistency of unwhipped double cream. To make a thicker sauce, reduce the quantity of milk by 150 ml (¼ pt). To make a thinner sauce, increase the quantity of milk by 150 ml (¼ pt).

35 g (1¼ oz) butter or margarine   METAL BLADE
25 g (1 oz) flour
450 ml (¾ pt) milk
1 bay leaf
Small piece onion
Small piece carrot
Salt
Pepper

1. Put the butter or margarine and flour in the processor bowl and process until they are well blended into a thick paste.
2. Combine the milk, bay leaf, onion and carrot in a heavy-based saucepan and season to taste with salt and pepper.
3. Bring the milk to boiling point, then reduce the heat and cook without a lid on the lowest possible setting for 15 minutes.
4. Strain the milk into a large jug or lipped bowl, then immediately switch on the machine and pour the milk through the feed tube while the motor is running.
5. Process until the sauce is smooth.

6. Rinse the saucepan in cold water and pour in the processed mixture.

7. Cook the sauce over gentle heat, stirring continuously until thickened, then cook for an additional minute.

Makes 450 ml (¾ pt)

BEEF AND BACON CRUMBLE

Provided that the top edges of the frying pan are flameproof the crumble can be completely cooked and browned in one utensil.

6 bacon rashers, rinds removed   METAL BLADE
15 ml (1 tbsp) vegetable oil
550 g (1¼ lb) lean beef, cut into 2.5 cm (1 in) cubes
1 beef stock cube
150 ml (¼ pt) hot water
5 ml (1 tsp) turmeric
5 ml (1 tsp) cornflour

For the topping:
175 g (6 oz) self-raising flour
Pinch salt
5 ml (1 tsp) baking powder
75 g (3 oz) butter or margarine

1. Switch on the machine and put the bacon-rashers through the feed tube, one at a time, while the motor is running.

2. Heat the oil in a large frying pan and stir in the bacon. Fry gently while processing the beef.

3. To chop the beef, place half the cubes in the bowl and pulse until chopped to the size of peas. Stir into the bacon mixture and raise the heat.

4. While the beef and bacon are frying, process the remaining meat. Stir this into the frying pan and cook for approximately 15 minutes, stirring occasionally until the meat is browned.

5. Crumble the stock cube into the hot water and stir into the meat mixture with the turmeric.

6. Add 150 ml (¼ pt) cold water blended with the cornflour and stir thoroughly, then cook over a low heat for about 15 minutes until the sauce thickens and the meat is tender.

7. Rinse and dry the processor bowl and blade. Reassemble and prepare the topping. Put the flour, salt and baking powder into the bowl and pulse once or twice to sift.

8. Add the butter (or margarine) cut into four pieces, then process continuously making sure that the pusher is in the feed tube.

9. When the flour mixture resembles fine breadcrumbs, spoon over the entire surface of the meat, pack down gently, then put the frying pan on the bottom rung under a medium grill for about 10 minutes until the crumble is cooked and golden.

If desired the meat mixture can be transferred to a flameproof tin or dish before the topping is added. Complete under the grill in the same way.

Serves 4 to 5

BEEF OLIVES

Beef olives is a traditional description of slices of meat filled with a stuffing and cooked in stock. Use a flameproof casserole so that it can be used for initially browning on the hob and then subsequent baking in the oven.

8 thin slices topside of beef   METAL BLADE
6 sprigs parsley   SLICING DISC
100 g (4 oz) fresh white bread, crusts removed
6 rashers bacon, derinded
40 g (1½ oz) soft margarine
1 size-4 egg
5 ml (1 tsp) mixed dried herbs
5 ml (1 tsp) lemon juice
Salt
Pepper
25 g (1 oz) seasoned flour
300 ml (½ pt) cold beef stock
2 medium onions, peeled and quartered

1. Thoroughly flatten the beef slices with a rolling pin or cleaver.
2. Attach the metal blade, switch on the machine and while the motor is running add the parsley followed by the bread torn into pieces, then the bacon one rasher at a time.
3. When the bacon is well chopped and with the motor running add 15 g (½ oz) of the margarine, the egg, herbs and lemon juice.
4. Remove the lid, add salt and pepper to taste and process briefly. The stuffing should be spreadable.
5. Remove the metal blade from the bowl and pile one-length of the stuffing along one edge of each meat slice and roll up fairly tightly.
6. Tie the beef olives with cotton in three or four places and dip into the seasoned flour. Shake off the surplus flour but do not throw it away.
7. Heat the remaining margarine in a flame-proof casserole and brown the beef on all sides.
8. Mix all the remaining flour with the stock and pour over the beef.
9. Fit the slicing disc in the processor bowl and slice the onions, using firm pressure on the pusher.

10. Add the onions to the casserole, cover with the lid and bake in a moderate oven, 180°C (350°F) Gas Mark 4, for 1 to 1½ hours until the beef is tender. Remove the cotton ties before serving.

Serves 8

BEEF STROGANOFF

If you wish to freeze the stroganoff omit the soured cream, stirring it in after thawing and reheating to serving temperature.

450 g (1 lb) fillet steak   SLICING DISC
2 medium onions, peeled and halved   (preferably
                                                                    thick)
175 g (6 oz) button mushrooms, stalks trimmed away
    close to the caps
50 g (2 oz) butter
5 ml (1 tsp) vegetable oil
2 tbsp tomato purée
Salt
Freshly ground black pepper
150 ml (¼ pt) soured cream
225 g (8 oz) long grain rice, freshly cooked and kept
    warm

1. Cut the steak into large pieces which will fit easily into the feed tube. Cover and chill in the freezer compartment of the refrigerator until firm but not solid.
2. Attach the slicing disc, insert a block of steak in the feed tube and use light pressure on the pusher while processing. Switch off between processing each piece.
3. Detach the lid, take out the sliced meat and set aside.
4. Replace the slicing disc and process the onions. Remove from the processor bowl as before.

5. Replace the slicing disc once more. Process the mushrooms into slices. There is no need to take especial care when placing them in the feed tube.

6. Melt the butter in a frying pan and sauté the onions until they are soft but not brown.

7. Stir in the mushrooms and cook for 2 to 3 minutes.

8. Remove the onions and mushrooms from the pan using a slotted spoon and set aside.

9. Reheat the butter and add the oil. Fry the steak briskly a few pieces at a time, turning them over so that all sides are sealed. Stir in the tomato purée and season to taste with salt and pepper, then return the onions and mushrooms to the pan.

10. When the mixture is thoroughly reheated switch off the heat and stir in the soured cream.

11. Arrange the hot rice on individual hot dinner plates and spoon the stroganoff on top.

Serves 4

CARROTTY PIE

This really is an old English recipe and is truly delicious.

Pastry
100 g (4 oz) plain flour   METAL BLADE
50 g (2 oz) butter   GRATING DISC
15 ml (1 tbsp) icing sugar, sifted
1 size-4 egg

Filling
50 g (2 oz) carrot
50 g (2 oz) crustless bread
2 egg yolks
1 egg white
150 ml (¼ pt) double cream

50 g (2 oz) butter, melted
15 ml (1 tbsp) brandy
15 ml (1 tbsp) orange flower water (obtainable from
the chemist)
1.25 ml (¼ tsp) freshly grated nutmeg
About 60 ml (4 tbsp) caster sugar

1. To make the pastry, first attach the metal blade then process all the ingredients together to form a pliable dough.
2. Roll out the pastry and use to line a 23 cm (8 in) loose-bottomed cake tin, lightly greased. You could use a 23 cm (8 in) flan ring on a baking tray if you prefer.
3. To make the filling, first remove the metal blade from the bowl and attach the grating disc. Process the carrots so that they are finely grated.
4. Remove the grating disc and attach the metal blade, pushing it well down to make sure that it is fixed in position.
5. Replace the lid, switch on the motor and add the bread in small pieces down the feed tube.
6. As soon as the breadcrumbs are completely incorporated and with the motor still running, add the egg yolks, egg white, cream, butter, brandy, orange flower water, nutmeg and half the sugar.
7. Process briefly, remove the lid and taste the mixture, then add the remaining sugar and blend if necessary.
8. Pour the filling into the uncooked pastry case and bake in a very moderate oven, 160°C (325°F) Gas Mark 3, for 45 to 50 minutes or until the filling has risen slightly and has acquired a golden crust.
9. Serve warm or cold.

Serves 6 to 8

CELERY AND APPLE SOUP

The apple is used unpeeled for extra colour in this delicate cream soup.

1 green dessert apple, washed,   METAL BLADE
    quartered and cored
1 head celery, trimmed and broken into 5 cm (2 in)
    lengths
50 g (2 oz) butter or soft margarine
50 g (2 oz) flour
600 ml (1 pt) milk
1.25 ml (¼ tsp) celery seed
450 ml (¾ pt) hot water
½ chicken stock cube, crumbled

1. Put the apple in the processor bowl, switch on the machine and add the celery through the feed tube while the motor is running. Process to a smooth purée.
2. Remove the lid and add the butter (or margarine) and flour to the celery purée. Process until blended although the mixture will not be completely smooth. Leave in the processor bowl.
3. Bring the milk to the boil in a large saucepan.
4. Switch on the machine and pour the hot milk into the processor bowl through the feed tube. Process to a purée.
5. Pour the mixture back into the saucepan and add the celery seed, 450 ml (¾ pt) hot water and the stock cube.
6. Cook over gentle heat, stirring frequently, for 45 minutes to 1 hour or until the soup has thickened.

Serves 6 to 8

CHEESE SOUFFLÉ

For a good soufflé egg whites should be stiffly but not over-beaten. Stiff dry beaten whites require too much mixing into the sauce, so limiting the chances of a good rise. The beater attachment will whisk egg whites sufficiently.

50 g (2 oz) plain flour	METAL BLADE
1.25 ml (¼ tsp) salt	WHISKING ATTACHMENT
1.25 ml (¼ tsp) ground white pepper	OPTIONAL
1.25 ml (¼ tsp) dry mustard powder	
50 g (2 oz) soft margarine	
300 ml (½ pt) milk	
3 size-2 eggs, separated	
100 g (4 oz) grated Cheddar cheese (page 44)	

1. Put the flour, salt, pepper and mustard in the processor bowl and pulse two or three times to sift.
2. Add the margarine, switch on the motor and pour the milk in rapidly through the feed tube. Process until the flour is incorporated and the margarine broken down into small particles.
3. Pour the sauce into a saucepan and bring to the boil, beating continuously. Reduce the heat and continue cooking for a further 2 to 3 minutes.
4. Remove the pan from the heat and leave to cool slightly.
5. Return the sauce to the processor bowl, add the egg yolks and the cheese and process until well mixed.
6. EITHER (a) beat the egg whites stiffly in a clean mixing bowl, then remove the processor lid, spoon the beaten egg whites on top of the sauce and pulse two or three times until just blended OR (b) transfer the sauce to a mixing bowl, wash and dry the processor bowl and beat the egg whites using the special attachment. Turn the egg whites on top of the sauce and fold in by hand.

7. Pour the soufflé mixture into a 1 litre (2 pt) greased soufflé dish, place on a metal baking sheet and bake in a pre-heated fairly hot oven, 195°C (375°F) Gas Mark 5, for 40 to 45 minutes or until well risen and golden on top.

8. Open the oven door carefully and take the soufflé to the table, moving slowly so as not to create a draught. Serve at once.

Serves 4

CHOUX PASTRY

Choux pastry is used for small buns, éclairs and gougère and these are usually baked. It is also mixed with other ingredients such as mashed potato and then deep fried. The basic recipe given here can be used for either sweet or savoury dishes. The most important point to note is that the boiling liquid must be poured into the flour as soon as it rises up the sides of the pan.

100 g (4 oz) plain flour   METAL BLADE
125 ml (¼ pt) water
50 g (2 oz) butter or margarine
2 size-4 eggs or 1½ size-2 eggs

1. Put the flour in the processor bowl.

2. Combine the water and butter or margarine in a saucepan and bring to the boil over gentle heat, stirring so that the water boils at the moment that the fat is fully melted.

3. Switch on the machine as soon as you see the boiling liquid rising up the sides of the saucepan and pour the liquid as quickly as possible through the feed tube while the motor is running. Process until smooth, when the ball of dough will start to draw away from the sides of the bowl.

4. Leave for a minute or two, then switch on the machine

and add the eggs one at a time through the feed tube until they are well incorporated and the mixture is no longer slimy. Use as required.

CREAM OF ONION SOUP

Use Spanish onions or ordinary small onions or choose the red-skinned onions for this soup when the colour will be slightly pink.

700 g (1½ lb) onions, peeled	METAL BLADE
50 g (2 oz) butter or margarine	
45 ml (3 tbsp) flour	
600 ml (1 pt) milk	
300 ml (½ pt) chicken stock	
1.25 ml (¼ tsp) bay leaf powder	
Salt	
Pepper	

1. Cut the onions into pieces which will drop easily through the feed tube and add to the processor while the machine is running. Switch off when finely chopped.
2. Melt the butter or margarine in a large saucepan, stir in the chopped onions and sauté until they are soft but not coloured.
3. Stir in the flour, then add the milk, stock, and bay leaf powder. Bring to the boil, stirring continuously, then season to taste with salt and pepper.
4. Cover the saucepan with the lid, reduce the heat and simmer the soup for 30 to 45 minutes or until the onion is very soft.
5. Purée the soup in the food processor. This may have to be done in two batches depending upon the capacity of the food processor bowl. Reheat the soup if necessary and adjust the seasoning.

Serves 6 to 8

DEWY FRUIT SALAD

This fruit salad has a really fresh tangy flavour and contains no added sugar. If you prefer a richer mixture, substitute soured cream for the yoghurt.

6 sweet biscuits (not creams), broken   METAL BLADE
25 g (1 oz) shelled hazelnuts   THICK SLICING DISC
1 large orange
1 firm pear
1 apple, Granny Smith or similar
1 large banana
90 ml (6 tbsp) natural yoghurt (or soured cream)

1. Attach the metal blade, place the broken biscuits in the processor bowl and pulse until roughly chopped but not pulverized. Remove the crumbs from the bowl and set aside.
2. Put the hazelnuts into the processor bowl and chop finely, scraping down the sides of the bowl once.
3. Leaving the hazelnuts in the bowl remove the metal blade and attach the slicing disc.
4. Peel the orange, removing as much of the pith as possible, then cut into quarters and remove the pips. Peel, quarter and core the pear. Without peeling, quarter and core the apple and peel the banana.
5. Process the fruit into thick slices, using only light pressure on the pusher. You may require to slice the fruit in batches.
6. Turn the mixture into a roomy serving dish, add the yoghurt (or soured cream) and turn rather than stir the fruit, so that the pieces are mixed but not mashed.
7. Sprinkle the reserved biscuits over the top.
8. Refrigerate for 30 minutes before serving.

Serves 4

FINNAN HADDIE SOUP

The Scottish Finnan Haddie has a delicate taste because of
the care with which it is smoked, but unless it is a special
occasion you will probably settle for smoked haddock.
The soup is more filling than may seem, so that only small
portions should be served if a substantial meal is to follow.

1 × 450 g (1 lb) smoked haddock   METAL BLADE
15 g (½ oz) butter
15 g (½ oz) flour
600 ml (1 pt) milk
15 ml (1 tbsp) fresh lemon juice
White pepper
Salt
60 ml (4 tbsp) double cream
5 ml (1 tsp) paprika

1. Put the haddock in a frying pan and pour over 300 ml
(½ pt) water. Poach gently until the fish is cooked, 5 to 10
minutes.
2. Remove the fish from the pan and strain the cooking
liquid into the processor bowl.
3. Add the butter to the liquid in the processor bowl and
blend briefly for the butter to melt, then add the flour and
half the milk and process until the mixture is smooth.
4. Remove the skin and bones and flake the fish flesh,
then add this to the mixture in the food processor.
5. Process until the mixture is well blended, then pour
into a large saucepan and stir in the remaining milk and
the lemon juice. Bring to the boil, then reduce the heat
and cook gently for 5 minutes.
6. Season with pepper and salt only if necessary, but it is
possible that the soup will be sufficiently salty.
7. Remove the pan from the heat, stir in the cream and
pour into a heated tureen or individual soup bowls.

8. Sprinkle paprika over the soup and serve hot.

Serves 6 to 7

INDIVIDUAL TURKEY AND PEPPER QUICHES

The pastry is sufficient for eight 10 cm (4 in) tartlet tins or two 25 cm (10 in) pastry cases, but you will need to increase the filling if using larger pastry shells because the proportion of filling to pastry is greater.

Pastry
350 g (12 oz) plain flour   METAL BLADE
Pinch salt
175 g (6 oz) butter or hard margarine, roughly cut
   into cubes
60 ml (4 tbsp) ice cold water
15 ml (1 tbsp) Worcestershire sauce

Filling
1 medium red pepper, deseeded and quartered
1 medium green pepper, deseeded and quartered
275 g (10 oz) cooked turkey
15 ml (1 tbsp) sautéd onion purée (page 194)
30 ml (2 tbsp) Worcestershire sauce
3 size-2 eggs
60 ml (4 tbsp) milk
5 ml (1 tsp) salt
150 ml (¼ pt) double cream
1.25 ml (¼ tsp) ground coriander

1. To make the pastry attach the metal blade.
2. Put the flour and salt into the process bowl and add the butter, spreading it out in a circle, and process until the mixture resembles fine breadcrumbs.

3. While the motor is running add 3 tablespoons of the water and the Worcestershire sauce and process until the dough just forms a ball. If the mixture is too dry add the remaining tablespoon of water, but do not be tempted to over-mix.

4. Turn the dough out on to a lightly floured work surface and knead until smooth.

5. Roll the dough out to 3 mm (⅛ in) thickness and cut out circles sufficiently large to line the tartlet tins. Remember that the dough will have to be bigger then the diameter of the tops of the tins.

6. Line the tins with the pastry, then fill each with a piece of foil covered with baking beans and bake blind in a fairly hot oven, 200°C (400°F) Gas Mark 6, for 15 to 20 minutes or until the pastry is just cooked.

7. Remove the foil and the baking beans and leave the pastry to cool in the tins.

8. To make the filling attach the metal blade. There is no need to wash the bowl between making the pastry and preparing the filling.

9. Switch on the machine and while the motor is running add the red and green peppers and when these are sufficiently chopped, add the turkey and all the other ingredients. Immediately switch off the machine and spoon the mixture into the pastry cases.

10. Bake in a moderately hot oven, 190°C (375°F) Gas Mark 5, for 20 minutes or until the quiches are set. Serve hot or cold.

Makes 8

JEWELLED BACON RISOTTO

Allow 50 g (2 oz) uncooked rice per person. The recipe here is for four portions but it can easily be doubled and the cooking time will not be appreciably longer.

600 ml (1 pt) well-flavoured   SLICING DISC
   chicken stock   METAL BLADE
225 g (8 oz) easy cook long grain rice
1 medium onion, peeled and halved
2 celery sticks, trimmed and broken into sizes to fit
   into the feed tube
1 medium green pepper, halved, cored and deseeded
1 medium red pepper, halved, cored and deseeded
25 g (1 oz) butter or margarine
8 lean back bacon rashers, derinded
30 ml (2 tbsp) frozen or canned peas
30 ml (2 tbsp) canned or frozen sweetcorn kernels
30 ml (2 tbsp) canned chick peas (or other beans)
30 ml (2 tbsp) sultanas

1. Heat the chicken stock in a large saucepan, stir in the rice, cover with a lid and set to cook over medium heat.

2. Attach the slicing disc to the processor bowl and process the onion, celery and peppers, using medium pressure on the pusher.

3. Melt the butter or margarine in a large frying pan and sauté the vegetables gently for 4 minutes.

4. Meanwhile remove the slicing disc, attach the metal blade and arrange the bacon rashers in the processor bowl. Pulse three or four times to chop the bacon roughly.

5. Stir the bacon into the sautéeing vegetables and continue cooking for a further 3 to 4 minutes or until the vegetables are tender and the bacon crispens.

6. Remove the vegetables and bacon with a slotted spoon and stir them into the rice cooking in the stock.

7. Add the remaining ingredients to the rice, remove the saucepan lid and cook for a further 4 to 5 minutes until all the liquid is absorbed. If you have cooked the rice over high heat the liquid may be absorbed before the rice

is cooked. Should this happen add more hot stock or boiling water for the remaining cooking time required.

Serves 4

MAYFAIR CARROTS

As the name suggests, this is an up-market way of cooking carrots so choose even-shaped carrots which will fit into the food processor tube without falling on their sides. You will then have nice round slices.

1 medium onion, peeled and halved   SLICING DISC
25 g (1 oz) unsalted butter
30 ml (2 tbsp) demerara sugar
Approx. 150 ml (¼ pt) well-flavoured chicken stock
450 g (1 lb) young carrots, peeled
Salt
Pepper
60 ml (4 tbsp) soured cream

1. Process the onion to thin slices.
2. Melt the butter in a heavy-based saucepan and sauté the onions gently until they are transparent.
3. Add the sugar, then cook constantly for 3 to 4 minutes until the onions are caramellized.
4. Stir in the stock thoroughly and bring to simmering point.
5. Meanwhile process the carrots into slices, add to the pan and cook without covering, but stirring from time to time, for 10 to 15 minutes or until the carrots are tender.
6. Season to taste with salt and pepper.
7. Stir in the cream, remove the pan from the heat and cover with a lid. Leave to stand for 2 or 3 minutes before turning into a serving dish.
8. Garnish with browned crumbs (page 36).

Serves 4

NORMANDY DEEP APPLE PANCAKE

This is an absolutely delicious dessert yet is economical to make. Although it can be cooked in one large frying pan it is easier to halve the mixture and to cook each pancake in a separate pan. The pancakes can then be turned over without any problems.

2 size-2 eggs, separated	METAL BLADE
75 g (3 oz) plain flour	SLICING DISC
100 g (4 oz) caster sugar	WHISK (OPTIONAL)
120 ml (8 tbsp) milk	
2.5 ml (½ tsp) vanilla essence	
450 g (1 lb) cooking apples	

Oil and butter for frying
Icing sugar for dusting

1. Put the egg whites into a large grease-free bowl and beat until stiff.
2. Attach the metal blade and put the flour, sugar, milk and vanilla essence into the processor bowl.
3. Switch on the machine and add the egg yolks through the feed tube. Process until blended.
4. Pour the batter into the beaten egg whites and fold in lightly with a tablespoon.
5. Remove the metal blade and attach the slicing disc to the processor bowl.
6. Peel, core and quarter the apples. Stack the apple pieces in the feed tube, insert the pusher, then slice in the food processor.
7. Mix the apples into the batter but do not overstir.
8. Heat a teaspoon of oil and a teaspoon of butter in each of two medium omelette pans or one large frying pan and when the fat is hot, pour in the batter. Immediately reduce the heat, cover with a lid and cook gently for 5

minutes until the pancake is golden underneath and the top nearly set.

9. Carefully turn the pancake over and cook uncovered for a further 5 minutes to brown the underside.

10. Transfer the pancake(s) to a heated serving dish and dust generously with icing sugar. Serve hot.

Serves 4

PARTY CHEDDAR HEDGEHOG

A mixture of cheeses shaped into a ball and coated in chopped dry-roasted peanuts. Place it in the centre of the cheese board and spike with cocktail sticks topped with gherkins, olives and tiny radishes. Serve in thin wedges with Melba toast.

100 g (4 oz) dry-roasted peanuts   METAL BLADE
225 g (8 oz) stale mature   FINE GRATING DISC
    Cheddar cheese
Walnut-sized piece onion
1 small carrot, peeled and halved
75 g (3 oz) cream cheese

For serving:
Cocktail sticks
Stoned olives, radishes, gherkins

1. Attach the metal blade, put the peanuts in the processor bowl and pulse until the nuts are finely chopped but not pulverized. Turn the nuts on to a shallow plate.

2. Remove the metal blade and attach the grating disc. Grate the cheese, onion and carrot into the processor bowl.

3. Remove the grating disc, replace the metal blade, making sure that it is pushed down and securely fixed. Add the cream cheese to the mixture in the processor bowl and pulse only until the mixture is lumpy.

4. Using a light touch gather the cheese into a ball, shape and coat with the chopped peanuts.

5. Chill in the refrigerator covered by an upturned bowl, then put the ball on a serving dish and spike with cocktail sticks topped with the olives, radishes and gherkins.

Serves 12 to 16

PEANUT-COATED HAMBURGERS IN TOMATO SAUCE

Although the peanuts make this a high-protein meal, they can be omitted if you wish but remember to add more salt to the burgers if you decide to do this.

Sauce

1 medium red pepper, cored   METAL BLADE
  and deseeded
1 medium onion, peeled
2.5 ml (½ tsp) dried oregano
2.5 ml (½ tsp) dried thyme
Pinch sugar
150 ml (¼ pt) tomato purée
150 ml (¼ pt) white wine
10 ml (2 tsp) Worcestershire sauce
Salt
Pepper

Hamburgers

2 medium onions, peeled
1 clove garlic, peeled
10 ml (2 tsp) French mustard

1 egg
30 ml (2 tbsp) parsley sprigs
Freshly ground black pepper
Salt
900 g (2 lb) trimmed braising steak, cut into 2.5 cm
   (1 in) cubes

350 g (12 oz) salted peanuts for coating
Oil for shallow frying

1. To prepare the sauce, first put the red pepper, cut into about four pieces, and the onion, cut into about four pieces, into the processor bowl and process until finely chopped. Scrape down the sides of the bowl once.

2. Spoon the mixture into a heavy-based saucepan and add the remaining ingredients and 150 ml (¼ pt) water.

3. Bring to the boil, then reduce the heat, cover with a lid to prevent spattering and cook very gently until the sauce has thickened, about 10 minutes.

4. While the sauce is cooking, prepare the hamburgers. Cut the onions up roughly and put into the processor bowl with the garlic and process until finely chopped, scraping down the sides of the bowl once.

5. Add the mustard, egg and parsley sprigs and season to taste with pepper and very sparingly with salt. Pulse once or twice to mix the ingredients.

6. With the motor running add the beef through the feed tube. If your food processor is small you will have to do this in batches completing the final mixing in a mixing bowl.

7. Turn the hamburger mixture on to a work surface, divide into twelve even pieces and shape into burgers.

8. Put the salted peanuts into the processor bowl. Insert the pusher in the feed tube and process until the nuts are finely chopped. Transfer to a dish or turn out onto a piece of greaseproof paper.

9. Coat the burgers with the salted peanuts pressing them well in with a palette knife.

10. Heat about 1 cm (½ in) oil in a frying pan and cook the burgers for 3 to 5 minutes on each side depending upon their thickness. Do not have the oil too hot or the nuts on the outside will burn while the inside remains raw.

11. Drain the burgers on kitchen paper, then serve with the sauce.

Makes 12 substantial burgers

PIPERADE

The posh name for scrambled eggs with onions, green peppers and tomatoes. Serve on toast as a breakfast or supper dish.

3 medium onions, peeled and halved   SLICING DISC
1 large clove garlic, peeled   METAL BLADE
45 ml (3 tbsp) vegetable oil
2 green peppers, cored, deseeded and halved
4 medium tomatoes, skinned (page 78)
4 size-2 eggs
Salt
Pepper

1. Attach the slicing disc and process the onions and garlic.

2. Heat the oil in a large frying pan and stir in the onions and garlic and fry gently for 5 to 10 minutes until the onions are soft.

3. While the onions are cooking process the peppers to thin slices.

4. Stir the peppers into the onions in the pan, cover with a lid, reduce the heat and cook for a further 5 minutes or until the peppers are crisp and tender.

5. While the vegetables are cooking remove the slicing disc and attach the metal blade. Place the tomatoes in the processor bowl and pulse 3 or 4 times to chop roughly. Stir into the sautéeing vegetables.

6. Switch on the food processor and while the motor is running add the eggs and seasoning through the feed tube and process briefly.

7. Remove the lid from the frying pan, stir in the egg mixture and continue stirring until the eggs are lightly scrambled. Serve at once.

Serves 4

PLAICE FILLETS IN ORANGE AND ONION SAUCE

Although fresh fish tastes better to me, frozen fillets can be used if you wish and any white fish could be substituted. Frozen fish must be thawed before using in this dish.

900 g (2 lb) fish fillets, skinned   METAL BLADE
½ bunch large spring onions, washed, trimmed and
    dried
1 × 5 cm (2 in) strip finely pared orange peel (thin
    outside skin only), cut into pieces
8 to 10 sprigs fresh parsley
50 g (2 oz) soft margarine or softened butter
30 ml (2 tbsp) fresh lemon juice
200 ml (½ pt) fresh orange juice (approx. 4 large
    oranges)
2.5 ml (½ tsp) white pepper
2.5 to 5 ml (½ to 1 tsp) salt
20 ml (4 tbsp) caster sugar
40 g (1½ oz) flour

1. Arrange the fish in a shallow greased baking dish.
2. Switch on the machine and while the motor is running

add the onions through the feed tube. Process until
roughly chopped, then remove them with a spoon and
spread over the fish.

3. Switch on the machine again and while the motor is
running add the orange peel and parsley through the feed
tube. Process until both are finely chopped.

4. Add the remaining ingredients either through the feed
tube or, if it is more convenient, place them directly in
the processor bowl, then process to a smooth sauce,
scraping down the sides of the bowl once. Pour the
frothy sauce over the fish and bake in a moderately hot
oven, 190°C (375°F) Gas Mark 5, for 25 to 30 minutes or
until the fish is cooked. Baste several times during cooking.

Serves 5 to 6

PORK CHOPS PEIRCEY

A small onion could be substituted for the shallot but
onions have a more pungent flavour which may mask the
taste of the peppers.

2 shallots, peeled   METAL BLADE
25 g (1 oz) butter or margarine
4 pork chops, trimmed
½ red pepper, cored, deseeded and halved
½ green pepper, cored, deseeded and halved
30 ml (2 tbsp) cornflour
2 shakes Tabasco
5 ml (1 tsp) lemon juice
150 ml (¼ pt) sweet cider
Salt
Pepper

1. Put the shallots into the processor bowl and process until finely chopped. Scrape down the sides of the bowl once during processing.
2. Melt the butter in a large frying pan and sauté the shallots until they are transparent.
3. Add the pork chops which should be trimmed of all fat and fry gently on each side for 5 to 10 minutes.
4. Draw the frying pan away from the heat and transfer the cooked pork chops to a warmed serving dish and keep hot.
5. Switch on the food processor and while the motor is running, add through the feed tube the peppers followed by the cornflour, Tabasco, lemon juice and cider. Process until smooth, scraping down the sides of the bowl once.
6. Pour the pepper purée into the shallots in the frying pan, return to the heat and bring to the boil, stirring all the time. Season to taste with salt and pepper.
7. Cook the sauce until it is thickened, then pour over the pork chops and serve at once.

Serves 4

RHUBARB AND APPLE COBBLER

This is a filling autumn pudding that I like to make with Bramley apples but it is an ideal recipe for using up the windfalls.

450 g to 550 g (1 to 1½ lb) cooking apples	SLICING DISC
	METAL BLADE
225 g (½ lb) rhubarb	
Approx. 90 ml (6 tbsp) demerara sugar	
225 g (8 oz) self-raising flour	
1.25 ml (¼ tsp) salt	
25 g (1 tsp) caster sugar	
50 g (2 oz) butter or margarine	

105 ml (7 tbsp) milk
Raspberry or strawberry jam

1. Prepare a fairly hot oven, 200°C (400°F) Gas Mark 6. Grease a 23 × 20.5 cm (9 × 8 in) rectangular or 25.5 cm (10 in) round oven-proof dish.
2. Attach the slicing disc. Peel, core and quarter the apples. Wash and trim the rhubarb and cut the sticks into lengths that will fit upright in the feed tube.
3. Process the apples and rhubarb into slices and put into the prepared dish with the demerara sugar, making sure to mix the sugar in evenly.
4. Remove the slicing disc, wipe out the processor bowl with kitchen paper to remove any excess moisture, then attach the metal blade. Put the flour, salt, caster sugar and the butter or margarine, cut into four pieces, into the bowl and process to coarse crumbs.
5. With the machine running add the milk through the feed tube, then switch off. Immediately inspect the dough which should be soft but manageable. Add more milk if necessary.
6. Turn the dough on to a floured working surface and roll out to a 25.5 × 20.5 cm (10 × 8 in) rectangle.
7. Spread the jam over the dough, leaving a 1 cm (½ in) border on the short sides and a 2.5 cm (1 in) border on the long side furthest away from you. Roll up firmly from the long jammed edge.
8. Using a sharp knife cut the dough into 1.5 cm (¾ in) slices.
9. Arrange the slices cut-side up on top of the fruit (it does not matter if there are small gaps between). Bake for 25 to 30 minutes or until the topping is well risen and golden brown. Serve hot with custard or whipped cream.

Serves 6

RHUBARB SUET PUDDING

It is no problem at all to shred the suet in the food processor but since most people like to use the packeted shredded suet, I have used it in this recipe. If you wish, the pudding can be cooked by pressure cooker or micro-wave.

225 g (8 oz) plain flour   METAL BLADE
110 g (4 oz) shredded suet   SLICING DISC
1 size-2 egg
Approx. 30 ml (2 tbsp) cold milk
750 g (1½ lb) rhubarb
Approx. 100 g (4 oz) demerara sugar

1. Attach the metal blade. Put the flour and suet into the processor bowl.
2. Switch on the machine and while the motor is running add the egg and half the milk through the feed tube. Process until the mixture forms a dough, then remove the lid and pinch the dough between finger and thumb when it should be· just firm enough to roll out. If the mixture is too stiff switch on the machine once more and add the remaining milk through the feed tube.
3. Cut off one-third of the dough and set aside; roll out the remainder on a floured work surface and fit it into a slightly greased 1.1 litre (2 pt) pudding basin so that the pastry protrudes about 1 cm (½ in) beyond the rim.
4. Roll out the remaining dough to a circle a little larger than the diameter of the basin. Set the pastry lid aside and cover with clingfilm or a teacloth to prevent it drying out.
5. Remove the metal blade and attach the slicing disc to the food processor. Rinse, dry and trim the rhubarb and cut into lengths to fit the feed tube. Using light pressure on the pusher process the rhubarb into slices.

6. Layer the rhubarb and sugar in the prepared pudding basin and fold the edges of the pastry over the fruit. Brush the pastry edges with water, then cover with the pastry lid. Pinch the edges of the pastry together well to prevent the juices escaping.

7. Grease one side of a piece of kitchen foil large enough to cover the basin, but before putting it in position, make a deep pleat down the centre. Wrap the foil securely round the sides of the basin, tying with string if necessary.

8. Put the basin on a trivet in a deep saucepan and pour boiling water between the basin and the saucepan until it reaches half-way up the basin.

9. Place the lid on the saucepan, bring to the boil, then reduce the heat to simmering point and steam for 2½ to 2¾ hours. Serve with old-fashioned Bird's custard.

Serves 5 to 6

SAUCE ÉSPAGNOLE

The basic brown sauce.

1 medium onion, peeled and quartered   METAL BLADE
1 carrot, scraped and cut into chunks
2 bacon rashers, rind and fat removed
50 g (2 oz) butter or margarine
100 g (4 oz) mushrooms, wiped
50 g (2 oz) plain flour
600 ml (1 pt) well-flavoured beef stock
2.5 ml (½ tsp) bay leaf powder
45 ml (3 tbsp) tomato purée
30 ml (2 tbsp) medium sherry
Salt
Pepper

1. Put the onion, carrot and bacon into the processor bowl and process until chopped.

2. Melt the butter or margarine in a large heavy-based saucepan and sauté the chopped vegetables and bacon, stirring constantly, for 10 minutes or until the onion browns.

3. Meanwhile put the mushrooms in the processor bowl and pulse until finely chopped.

4. Add the flour to the sautéed vegetables and bacon in the pan and cook for 2 minutes, stirring continuously, until the flour browns.

5. Stir in the mushrooms, stock, bay leaf powder, tomato purée and sherry and season to taste with salt and pepper.

6. Bring the mixture to the boil, then reduce the heat, cover with a lid and simmer for 30 minutes. Stir frequently during cooking to prevent sticking.

7. Pour half the sauce into the processor bowl. Insert the pusher in the feed tube and process until smooth, scraping down the sides of the bowl once. Pour into another bowl or pan.

8. Process the remaining sauce, mix with the first batch and gently reheat.

Makes 600 ml (1 pt).

SAUTÉED ONION PURÉE

Prepare the purée at your leisure, spoon into screw-top jars and cover with a disc of waxed paper or cellophane before putting the lid on. I find baby food jars just the right size and the lids are particularly good because they do not get damaged when first removed. Use the purée whenever you need to add sautéed onion flavouring to a savoury dish. The recipe can be doubled if your food processor bowl is large enough to purée the mixture at one time.

225 g (½ lb) small onions, peeled   SLICING DISC
    and halved   METAL BLADE
50 g (2 oz) butter

1.   Attach the slicing disc and process the onions thinly.
2. Melt the butter in a saucepan, then sauté the onions for about 5 minutes until they are golden brown.
3. Remove the pan from the heat and leave the onions to cool.
4. Remove the slicing disc from the processor bowl and fit the metal blade.
5. Place the sautéed onions in the processor bowl and process until puréed, scraping down the sides of the bowl twice.
6. Spoon the purée into one or two small jars. Cover and close securely.

The purée will keep in the refrigerator for about 4 weeks or in the freezer for up to 2 months.

Makes abou: 200 g (7 oz)

SAVOURY STUFFED CHOUX BUNS

Choux pastry   METAL BLADE
100 g (4 oz) plain flour
125 ml (¼ pt) water
50 g (2 oz) butter
2 size-4 eggs or 1½ size-2 eggs

Filling
15 g (½ oz) butter or margarine
100 g (4 oz) chicken livers, rinsed, trimmed and
    patted dry between sheets of kitchen paper
1.25 ml (¼ tsp) dried rosemary
100 g (4 oz) Philadelphia cream cheese
Salt
Pepper

1. Prepare the choux pastry following the method on page 175.
2. Place teaspoonsful of the mixture well spaced out on greased baking trays and bake in a fairly hot oven, 200°C (400°F) Gas Mark 6, for about 20 minutes or until the buns are well risen, deep golden brown and crisp on the outside. If your oven has a see-through door and the pastry seems to be darkening after the first 15 minutes, reduce the temperature for the remaining cooking time by one setting. Try not to open the oven door during baking.
3. Transfer the buns to a wire rack and pierce the sides immediately to let out any steam. Leave to cool.
4. While the pastry is baking, prepare the filling. If you have scraped out the bowl sufficiently well, there will be no need to wash it first. Melt the butter in a saucepan over medium heat and fry the chicken livers, stirring constantly until they are opaque. Stir in the rosemary and cook, stirring, for a few more moments. Leave to cool.
5. Put the sautéed liver mixture in the processor bowl and add the cheese and seasoning to taste. Process until well blended, scraping down the sides of the bowl once.
6. Using a teaspoon fill the buns with the chicken mixture, arrange on a platter and serve within 2 hours.

Makes 24

SLIMMER'S VEGETABLE SOUP

Fortunately low calorie soups don't have to taste as though they are especially prepared for slimmers, so all the family can enjoy them. You may find that you have to process the vegetables in batches.

450 g (1 lb) onions, peeled and quartered	SLICING DISC METAL BLADE
1 green pepper, quartered, cored and deseeded	

½ head celery, trimmed
225 g (½ lb) carrots, peeled
1 × 396 g (14 oz) can tomatoes
1 clove garlic, peeled
15 ml (1 tbsp) dried parsley
60 ml (4 tbsp) sliced beans
Salt
Pepper
Dash Worcestershire sauce

1. Attach the slicing disc and process the onions, green
pepper, celery and carrots.
2. Remove the disc and place the sliced vegetables in a
large saucepan.
3. Attach the metal blade and purée the tomatoes and
garlic.
4. Add this mixture to the vegetables.
5. Stir in the parsley and beans.
6. Add boiling water to cover the vegetables. Put the pan
over the heat then bring to the boil.
7. Reduce the heat, cover the saucepan and simmer for
about 1 hour, stirring occasionally, or until the vegetables
are cooked.
8. Season with salt and pepper and add a dash of Worcestershire sauce if you wish.

If you prefer a smooth soup attach the metal blade and
purée the soup in three or four lots.

Serves 8

STEAK DIANE

Traditionally the steaks should be not more than 1 cm
(½ in) thick and are usually medium cooked rather than
rare.

¼ onion   METAL BLADE
8 sprigs fresh parsley
15 ml (1 tsp) fresh lemon juice
30 ml (2 tbsp) Worcestershire sauce
25 g (1 oz) butter
30 ml (2 tbsp) vegetable oil
4 fillet steaks, beaten to 1 cm (½ in) thick
15 ml (1 tbsp) double cream

1. Put the onion, parsley, lemon juice and Worcestershire sauce in the processor bowl and process to a purée, scraping down the sides of the bowl once.
2. Heat the butter and oil in a large frying pan and fry the steaks for 2 to 2½ minutes on each side.
3. Remove the steaks to a heated serving dish, add the puréed onion to the juices remaining in the pan and cook for 2 minutes, stirring continuously until the mixture boils.
4. Season the juices to taste with salt and pepper, then remove the pan from the heat.
5. Stir in the cream and pour over the steaks.

Serves 4

STUFFED MARROW

Marrow has a special plus because it is low in calories. Choose the leanest possible beef for a real slimmer's meal.

1 × 900 g (2 lb) marrow   METAL BLADE
1 small onion, peeled
15 ml (1 tbsp) vegetable oil
450 g (1 lb) lean beef, trimmed and cubed
45 ml (3 tbsp) tomato purée
2.5 ml (½ tsp) Worcestershire sauce
1.25 ml (¼ tsp) ground allspice
15 ml (1 tbsp) flour

300 ml (½ pt) hot well-flavoured beef stock
Salt
Pepper

For garnish:
Deep fried onion rings

1. Peel the marrow and cut in half lengthwise. Using a sharp knife scoop out the seeds and pith, leaving a hollow.
2. Simmer the marrow halves in a large pan of boiling salted water until just tender. Drain carefully so that the marrow remains intact.
3. Place the marrow, hollow side underneath, in a colander to remove all surplus liquid.
4. Put the onion in the processor bowl and pulse until finely chopped.
5. Heat the oil in a large frying pan and sauté the onion gently until soft but not brown. Draw the pan away from the heat.
6. Switch on the food processor and drop the meat cubes through the feed tube while the motor is running. Switch off as soon as the last piece has been added. You may have to do this in two batches depending on the capacity of the processor bowl.
7. Put the frying pan over fierce heat and add the meat a handful at a time, stirring briskly until the meat is browned. Drain off all the fat. It is better to do this away from the heat to avoid the danger of the fat catching fire as it is spooned away.
8. Stir the tomato purée, Worcestershire sauce and allspice into the meat mixture, then stir in the flour.
9. Add the beef stock and season with salt and pepper. Bring to the boil, reduce the heat, cover with the lid and simmer for 25 to 35 minutes or until the mixture has thickened and is no longer runny. Stir frequently during cooking to prevent sticking.

10. Put the marrow halves into a roasting tin hollow-side up and fill with the meat mixture.

11. Cover the roasting tin securely with foil and bake in a moderately hot oven 190°C (375°F) Gas Mark 5 for 20 to 30 minutes or until the marrow is soft.

12. Transfer the marrow to a heated serving dish and decorate with the fried onion rings.

Serves 4

WHITE SAUCE SUITABLE FOR COATING

The recipe cannot be made in smaller quantities but the sauce will keep in a covered container in the refrigerator for a few days and it will also freeze.

50 g (2 oz) flour   METAL BLADE
50 g (2 oz) butter or margarine
600 ml (1 pt) milk
Salt
Pepper

1. Put the flour and butter or margarine into the processor bowl and process until the mixture forms a paste.

2. Bring the milk to the boil, switch on the machine and while the motor is running pour in the milk through the feed tube.

3. Process until the sauce is smooth. It will not be thick at this stage.

4. Rinse the saucepan in cold water and pour in the processed sauce, then cook, stirring constantly, over gentle heat for 3 minutes until the sauce has thickened. Season to taste with salt and pepper and at this stage add any other flavourings.

Makes 600 ml (1 pt)

COMBINATION RECIPES

Choose your recipe, buy or collect the ingredients, then let your food processor prepare the component parts at any convenient time, storing them appropriately.

A wide variety of ingredients can be stored for several weeks, particularly if you have a freezer. So, if you have a special preference, say, for cheesey dishes, you can buy in bulk, grate the lot, then either weigh and pack it in appropriate quantities, or freeze it in a large sealed container.

When you are ready to cook, assemble the ingredients. Mix them in the food processor where applicable and then all you have to do is cook. This cuts the preparation time very considerably. No washing, peeling, scraping, grating, chopping or slicing to do at the last minute.

ALMOND RICE DARIOLES WITH PUERTO RICAN SAUCE

Plain boiled rice can be made into a super starter when served with a special sauce such as this. If you do not have dariole moulds, small 5 cm (2 in) Tupperware pots can be used.

350 g (12 oz) boiled rice   METAL BLADE
60 ml (4 tbsp) paprika vinaigrette (page 72)
75 g (3 oz) chopped blanched almonds (page 28)
Salt
Pepper
1 walnut-size piece of onion
1 canned pimento
2 medium tomatoes, skinned, halved and deseeded
30 ml (2 tbsp) orange juice
15 ml (1 tbsp) lemon juice
75 ml (2½ fl oz) thick mayonnaise (page 127)
50 g (2 oz) peeled cooked prawns

For garnish:
6 prawns

Mix the rice, vinaigrette and almonds together in a mixing bowl and season with salt and pepper. Press the mixture into six dariole moulds and refrigerate for 30 to 60 minutes. Put the onion into the processor bowl, switch on the motor and add the pimento and tomatoes through the feed tube, followed by the orange and lemon juice. Remove the lid, scrape down the sides of the bowl and add the mayonnaise and prawns. Pulse only until the mayonnaise is combined and the prawns roughly chopped. Season to taste with salt and pepper if necessary. Turn the moulds out on to a cool serving dish and spoon the sauce around them. Top each rice mould with a prawn.

Serves 6

BACON PIZZA TOPPING

Use on a scone or yeast dough.

Pizza scone mix made from 225 g (8 oz) self-raising
   flour
A little vegetable oil
60 ml (4 tbsp) tomato purée
5 ml (1 tsp) mixed dried herbs
50 g (2 oz) grated Cheddar cheese (page 44)
3 rashers lean bacon, derinded and coarsely chopped
   (page 32)
2 firm tomatoes, sliced (page 78)

Roll out the scone mix to a 28 cm (11 in) circle, place on a
greased and floured baking tin and brush the rim with
vegetable oil. Spread the base with the tomato purée
and sprinkle with the herbs. Arrange the cheese evenly on
top, cover with the tomato slices and sprinkle with the
chopped bacon. Bake in a hot oven, 220°C (425°F) Gas
Mark 7, for 20 to 25 minutes.

Serves 2 to 4

BREAST OF CHICKEN SAUCE CHAMPIGNONS

If you wish you can substitute natural yoghurt for single
cream to reduce the richness of the delicious mushroom
sauce.

4 boneless chicken breasts, skinned
Salt
Pepper
Juice of 1 lemon
50 g (2 oz) butter or margarine
1 small onion, peeled and sliced (page 63)

350 g (12 oz) button mushrooms, sliced (page 62)
60 ml (4 tbsp) chicken stock *OR* water and ⅛ stock
  cube
60 ml (4 tbsp) dry white wine
10 ml (2 tsp) cornflour
150 ml (¼ pt) single cream

Remove the stringy white tendons and partially flatten the chicken pieces with a rolling pin or cleaver. Sprinkle both sides of the chicken breasts with salt, pepper and lemon juice. Melt the butter or margarine in a heavy-based frying pan and sauté the chicken for 10 to 15 minutes or until cooked, turning the chicken pieces over half-way through cooking. Transfer the chicken to a serving casserole, cover and keep warm. Stir the onions and mushrooms into the juices in the frying pan and cook until the onion is soft. Add the stock and wine, raise the heat and cook, stirring continuously, until the mixture thickens and becomes sticky. Stir the cornflour into the cream, then reduce the heat and add the mixture to the frying pan, stirring until the sauce thickens slightly. Adjust the seasoning, remove the casserole lid, pour the sauce over the chicken and serve at once.

Serves 4

CARROT AND ORANGE SALAD

A family or party salad which can be increased in quantity. It is advisable to eat this salad within 24 hours of preparation.

2 medium oranges   METAL BLADE
450 g (1 lb) carrots, peeled   GRATING DISC
50 g (2 oz) raisins
150 ml (¼ pt) mayonnaise (page 127)

Cut a slice from the top and the bottom of each orange so
that they will stand firmly on a chopping board. Using a
sharp knife cut down along the contour to remove the rind
and pith. Slice one of the oranges thinly and set aside for
garnish. Holding the second orange over the processor
bowl to catch the juice, with a sharp knife remove the
segments, leaving the thin membrane intact. As you work
drop the slices into the food processor bowl and then
squeeze the orange core in your hand to release the
remaining juice. Add the raisins and mayonnaise. Process
briefly to mix, then remove the metal blade. Attach the
grating disc and grate the carrots on to the mixture.
Remove the processor bowl from the spindle, take out the
disc and, using a spoon, mix the carrots with the mayonnaise. Spoon the salad into an attractive dish and garnish
with overlapping circles of the reserved orange. Cover and
keep in a cool place until required.

Serves 6 to 8

CELERY AND CARROT MUSTARD CREAM SALAD

If you have a chipper disc use this for slicing the carrots
(page 43). Otherwise use the slicing disc.

60 ml (4 tbsp) mayonnaise (page 127)   SLICING DISC
30 ml (2 tbsp) Dijon mustard
30 ml (2 tbsp) soured cream
3 celery stalks, washed, trimmed and cut into pieces
   to fit vertically into the feed tube.
175 g (6 oz) carrot, peeled and cut into pieces to fit
   horizontally into the feed tube.

Put the mayonnaise, mustard and soured cream into the
processor bowl and attach the slicing disc. Pack the celery
vertically into the feed tube and process until sliced. Pack

the carrots horizontally into the feed tube against the disc
and process into long thin slices. Remove the bowl and
disc. Use a spoon to mix the vegetables and sauce
together. Turn the salad into a serving dish. Cover and
chill until required.

Serves 4 as a side salad

CHICKEN PAPRIKA

Choose a heavy-based flameproof casserole or saucepan
large enough to take a whole chicken. I have included this
recipe to make a change from the traditional method of
roasting in the oven.

   1 × 1.6 to 1.8 kg (3½ to 4 lb) oven-ready chicken
   Salt
   Pepper
   30 ml (2 tbsp) paprika
   15 ml (1 tbsp) vegetable oil
   6 rashers streaky bacon, derinded and chopped (page
      32)
   1 large onion, peeled and finely chopped (page 63)
   100 g (4 oz) carrots, peeled and sliced (page 42)
   1 large red pepper, deseeded and chopped (page 67)
   2.5 ml (½ tsp) chilli compound powder
   10 ml (2 tsp) cornflour
   150 ml (¼ pt) soured cream
   50 ml (1 tbsp) freshly chopped parsley (page 57)

Rub the surface of the chicken with salt, pepper and the
paprika. Heat the oil in a large heavy-based casserole or
saucepan. Brown the chicken on all sides, then lift it out
carefully and set aside. Add the bacon and onion to the
pan and sauté until soft, then mix in the carrots, pepper
and the chilli compound powder. Add about 300 ml (½ pt)

boiling water. Place the chicken on top of the vegetables breast-side uppermost. Cover tightly with the lid, reduce the heat and cook gently for 1 to 1½ hours until the chicken is tender and thoroughly cooked. Lift the chicken from the pan, allowing the juices from the cavity to drain on to the vegetables, and transfer to a heated deep serving dish. Cut the chicken into joints if you wish. Blend the cornflour with 2 tablespoons cold water and mix into the vegetables. Bring to the boil to thicken the mixture, then remove from the heat and stir in the cream and parsley. Either pour the vegetable mixture around the chicken in the dish or purée in the food processor (page 71) and serve separately.

Serves 6

CRUSTY HERBY FRENCH BREAD

So many herb and garlic breads have soft crusts when served. I think you will find this one pleasantly crusty. Increase the quantity as many times as you like and bake all the loaves in the oven at the same time.

For each French loaf:
100 g (4 oz) butter   METAL BLADE
15 ml (1 tbsp) mixed chopped fresh herbs (page 57)
Pinch garlic salt

Prepare a hot oven, 200°C (400°F) Gas Mark 6. While the oven is heating make diagonal cuts in the bread at approximately 2.5 cm (1 in) intervals – take care that you do not cut through the bottom crust. Put the butter, herbs and garlic salt into the processor bowl and process until well blended. Spread the cut sides of the bread with the mixture, making sure that it is well pressed down. Reassemble the loaf, pressing the slices together. Wrap each loaf separately in foil and bake for 15 minutes, then open the foil and continue baking for a further 5 to 10 minutes until the crust is crisp.

Each small French loaf serves 4 to 6

CRUSTY WALNUT PULL LOAF

An unusual way of turning an ordinary brown loaf into a tea-time treat. It is a real diet-killer and can be eaten with fork or fingers. Serve with a finger bowl of cold lemony water.

1 small rectangular wholemeal loaf   METAL BLADE
100 g (4 oz) unsalted butter
175 g (6 oz) demerara sugar
50 g (2 oz) coarsely chopped walnuts (page 63)

Cut off all the crusts from the bread and use for making breadcrumbs in another recipe (page 36). Using a sharp knife, make one deep cut along the centre of the length of the loaf and three equidistant cross-wise cuts (do not cut the loaf all the way through). Put the loaf in a shallow baking tin or ovenproof dish. Put the butter and sugar in the processor bowl and process until creamy. Spread the mixture all over the bread and into the cuts. Sprinkle the top of the loaf with half the nuts and press the remainder into the sides. Bake in a moderately hot oven, 190°C (375°F) Gas Mark 5, for 15 minutes or until the sugary mixture begins to bubble. Using two fish slices transfer the loaf carefully (remember the syrup will be very hot) on to a wooden board. The sections may open during baking but this makes the bread crunchier. Leave to cool for a few moments, then pull the sections apart and serve with freshly whipped cream. Spoon any remaining nuts on top if you wish.

Serves 8

CYPRUS CAKE

The cake is reminiscent of one which I had in Cyprus made from semolina and soaked in cinnamon syrup.

175 g (6 oz) butter or margarine   METAL BLADE
175 g (6 oz) caster sugar
4 size-2 eggs
225 g (8 oz) fine semolina
5 ml (1 tsp) ground cinnamon
100g (4 oz) finely chopped blanched almonds (page 28)

For the syrup:
100 g (4 oz) granulated sugar
5 ml (1 tsp) lemon juice
2.5 ml (½ tsp) ground cinnamon or 1 cinnamon stick

Cut the butter or margarine into four or six pieces, place in the processor bowl and process until smooth. Remove the lid and add the caster sugar, eggs, semolina and cinnamon and process for 30 seconds. Scrape down the sides of the bowl, then process for 10 to 15 seconds until the mixture is smooth. During the last few seconds and while the machine is still running, add the chopped nuts through the feed tube. Turn the cake mixture into a well-greased 25.5 × 20.5 cm (10 × 8 in) roasting or Swiss roll tin. Smooth the top of the batter with a palette knife and bake in a moderate oven, 180°C (350°F) Gas Mark 4, for 35 to 40 minutes or until the cake is well risen but only pale golden on the top. Leave the cake in the tin while making the syrup.

Put the granulated sugar and lemon juice in a medium saucepan, add 150 ml (¼ pt) water and stir until the sugar has dissolved. Add the cinnamon or cinnamon stick. Cook over medium heat until the mixture boils, then simmer for 5 minutes until a thin syrup is formed. (Do not overcook the syrup because if it is too thick it will form a crust on top of the cake.) Pour the hot syrup over the still hot cake and make holes through the cake with a skewer so that the syrup will be able to seep and soak in more easily. Serve warm or cold straight from the tin.

Makes 20 to 30 pieces

EGG AND ANCHOVY SAUCE

300 ml (½ pt) simple white sauce   METAL BLADE
  (page 144)
1 hard-boiled egg
2 anchovy fillets

Heat the sauce and pour into the processor bowl. Switch on the machine and add the egg and anchovies through the feed tube. Pulse until the egg is roughly chopped, then process continuously until the egg and anchovy is blended into the sauce. Scrape down the sides of the bowl once during processing.

Makes 300 ml (½ pt)

EGG AND ONION PÂTÉ

How often do you make excuses for not inviting guests because it is all too much trouble? Why not have a pâté party which is so easy to prepare using the food processor. Include this recipe in your repertoire.

6 hard-boiled eggs   METAL BLADE
1 quarter small onion
90 ml (6 tbsp) mayonnaise (page 127)
2.5 ml (½ tsp) fresh lemon juice
150 ml (¼ pt) prepared aspic jelly, cooled
Salt
Pepper

Cut the eggs in half and arrange them in a circle in the processor bowl. Switch on the machine and drop the onion through the feed tube while the motor is running. Switch off, pour the mayonnaise, lemon juice and 5 tablespoons of the cooled aspic jelly through the feed tube, add a little salt and pepper and process to a smooth paste. Taste and adjust seasoning, then spoon the mixture into individual dishes and pour a little of the remaining aspic jelly over each. If the aspic has become set, warm it gently over a bowl of steaming hot water. Chill the pâté before serving.

Serves 4

FRUIT STUFFING

This recipe can be used for pork, veal or lamb. The mixture is sufficient to fill a boned leg of lamb.

1 medium onion, peeled   METAL BLADE
6 thin slices crustless bread
25 g (1 oz) butter or margarine
5 ml (1 tsp) thyme leaves

2.5 ml (½ tsp) pulverized rosemary leaves (page 57)
Juice and grated rind of 1 large orange
Juice and grated rind of ½ lemon
75 g (3 oz) raisins
75 g (3 oz) sultanas
Salt
Pepper
1 egg

Cut the onion into quarters, place in the bowl and process until finely chopped. While the motor is still running, add the bread, torn into pieces, through the feed tube. As soon as the bread forms coarse crumbs add the butter or margarine, herbs, fruit juices and grated rinds. Remove the lid and add the raisins and sultanas, process briefly and add salt and pepper to taste. Lastly add the egg and process to a firm stuffing consistency.

Serves 6 to 8

ICED CHEESE

Pretty little potted cheeses to serve at a buffet party or as an after-dinner savoury. Egg cups or 60 ml (2 oz) Tupperware pots can be used in place of metal dariole moulds.

50 g (2 oz) unsalted butter, cut into   METAL BLADE
    four pieces
60 ml (4 tbsp) thick Béchamel sauce (page 166), cold
45 ml (3 tbsp) single cream
225 g (8 oz) Cheshire cheese, grated (page 44)
6 round cheese biscuits

For garnish:
2 to 4 large radishes, sliced (page 71)
Shredded lettuce and watercress leaves

Put the butter, sauce and cream in the processor bowl and process until creamy. Open the lid, add half the cheese and process until mixed evenly. Uncover once more, add the remaining cheese and process to a smooth creamy paste, scraping down the sides of the bowl once. Divide the mixture between six small dariole moulds. Press down the cheese paste gently, then smooth the tops with a round-bladed knife. Cover the moulds and chill in the freezer until firm.

To unmould, dip the darioles into hot water, making sure the water does not come over the rim. Turn the iced cheeses on to individual biscuits, then decorate the tops with radish slices. Arrange the biscuits on a platter and intersperse with the shredded lettuce and watercress leaves.

Serves 6

INDIVIDUAL ONION QUICHES

If you do not already have individual flan tins this recipe can be made into one large quiche, but it really is worth going out to buy the smaller tins as they look so very pretty whether you are serving them as a starter or as a supper dish. The individual flan tins have a diameter of about 10 cm (4 in) and are usually fluted.

175 g (6 oz) short crust pastry (page 142)
30 ml (2 tbsp) soft margarine or butter
225 g (8 oz) onions, peeled and sliced (page 63)
1 size-2 egg
150 ml (¼ pt) single cream
Salt
Pepper
50 g (2 oz) grated Cheddar cheese (page 44)

Divide the pastry into four even pieces and roll out each piece to a 15 cm (6 in) round. Gently ease the pastry into the greased tins taking care that it is not stretched. Press the sides of the pastry into the fluted border. Run the rolling pin across the top of the tins to remove any surplus pastry and you will find that the pastry is thicker round these edges. Prepare a fairly hot oven, 200°C (400°F) Gas Mark 6. Bake blind for 15 minutes using foil or paper and baking beans to prevent the centre of the pastry from rising.

While the pastry cases are baking, melt the fat in a pan and sauté the onions until they are soft but not coloured. Beat the egg and cream together either by hand or in the food processor and season to taste with salt and pepper.

Remove the pastry from the oven and take out the foil or paper and baking beans. Reduce the oven temperature to 180°C (350°F) Gas Mark 4. Spread the cheese into the base of the pastry cases, cover with the onion which should be transferred with a slotted spoon. Pour the egg and cream mixture over the top and return the tins to the oven. Bake for 25 to 35 minutes or until the custard is set and a golden colour. Serve hot or cold.

Serves 4

INMACULADA'S COOKIES

These round nut-coated biscuits are from a recipe given to me by my Spanish friend.

100 g (4 oz) soft butter or margarine   METAL BLADE
50 g (2 oz) caster sugar
1 egg yolk
5 ml (1 tsp) vanilla essence
1.25 ml (¼ tsp) almond essence

100 g (4 oz) plain flour
1 egg white, slightly beaten
75 g (3 oz) finely chopped almonds (page 28)

Put the butter or margarine, sugar, egg yolk, vanilla and almond essences into the processor bowl and process until smooth. Remove the lid, add the flour and process until just combined. Refrigerate for 30 minutes. Shape the mixture into tiny balls about 1 cm (½ in) in diameter, then dip in the beaten egg white and press in the chopped nuts. Place the cookies, well spaced out, on ungreased baking trays and flatten with a fork. Bake in a moderately hot oven, 190°C (375°F) Gas Mark 5, for 8 to 10 minutes or until golden brown. If one tray seems to be cooking more slowly than the others, change their places during cooking. It will not be harmful if you open the oven door. When the biscuits are cooked remove them from the baking tray and cool on a wire rack.

Makes about 30

LAMB WITH APRICOT STUFFING

Ask the butcher to bone the lamb for you or, if you are doing it yourself, use a very sharp knife to loosen the flesh close to the blade bone. You will then have to cut at the socket joint before you can remove the bone. Loosen and remove the other bones in the same way.

1 × 1.8 kg (4 lb) shoulder of lamb,   METAL BLADE
   boned
15 g (½ oz) dripping or lard
1 medium onion, peeled and sliced (page 63)
1 carrot, peeled and sliced (page 42)
1 bay leaf
300 ml (½ pt) stock made from lamb bones

Stuffing
100 g (4 oz) dried apricots, soaked overnight
50 g (2 oz) fresh breadcrumbs (page 36)
25 g (1 oz) chopped walnuts (page 63)
1 small onion, peeled and finely chopped (page 63)
1 size-4 egg
Salt
Pepper

First prepare the stuffing. Drain the apricots thoroughly and put into the processor bowl. Pulse until finely chopped, then add the remaining ingredients and process until well blended. Press the stuffing evenly into the lamb cavities, then roll up and tie securely in several places with string.

Preheat a moderate oven 180°C (350°F) Gas Mark 4. Melt the fat in a large roasting dish and then, when it is hot, put in the lamb, turning the joint over to coat it evenly. Add the vegetables and the bay leaf, then pour the stock over the lamb. Cover the tin with a piece of foil and bake for 1½ to 1¾ hours until the meat is tender. Take the joint out of the tin and cut away the string. Place the meat on a serving dish and keep warm. Skim the fat from the juices in the tin and take out the bay leaf. Purée the remaining juices and vegetables in the food processor, then reheat and pour over the lamb.

Serves 6 to 8

MAMA'S MANICOTTI

The cheese filling goes well with the tomato sauce but you could ring the changes. Try a prawn filling and anchovy sauce or add ham to the ricotta and top with an éspagnole sauce. To save waste gather the trimmings together, reroll and cut.

One recipe Home-made Pasta (page 119)
One recipe Ricotta Filling for Pasta (page 138)
One recipe Tomato Sauce (page 151)

Roll the pasta out thinly to the thickness of a 5p piece and
cut into 12.5 × 7.5 cm (5 × 3 in) rectangles. Place a
'sausage' of the ricotta filling along one long edge of each
piece of pasta, leaving a 1 cm (½ in) uncovered border at
either end. Starting at the filled edge, roll up each piece of
pasta and arrange them close together in a shallow dish.
Pour the tomato sauce over, cover the dish with a lid or
sheet of foil and bake in a fairly hot oven, 200°C (400°F)
Gas Mark 6, for 30 to 35 minutes.

Makes 12; Serves 4 to 6

NEW ENGLAND LAYER CAKE

Vegetable oil rather than butter or margarine is used in
this recipe so that the method of mixing is slightly
different. The cake is exceptionally moist and the icing has
a pronounced lemon flavour.

175 g (6 oz) dark soft brown sugar   METAL BLADE
2 size-2 eggs
150 g (5 oz) finely grated carrot (page 42)
50 g (2 oz) blanched chopped almonds (page 28)
200 ml (7 fl oz) vegetable oil (corn oil gives a nice
    flavour)
Pinch salt
2.5 ml (½ tsp) bicarbonate of soda
2.5 ml (½ tsp) cinnamon
1.25 ml (¼ tsp) ground cardamom
175 g (6 oz) plain flour

Icing
75 g (3 oz) cream cheese
5 ml (1 tsp) fresh lemon juice
5 ml (1 tsp) grated lemon rind
175 g (6 oz) icing sugar, sifted
25 g (1 oz) blanched chopped almonds (page 28)

Put the sugar in the processor bowl, switch on the machine and while the motor is running add the eggs one at a time through the feed tube. As soon as the mixture is creamy add the grated carrots and nuts through the feed tube and gradually pour in the oil. Remove the lid and add the salt, bicarbonate of soda and spices and process until these are incorporated. Remove the lid once more and sprinkle half the flour over the surface, then pulse three or four times until the flour is incorporated. Repeat with the remaining flour. Turn the mixture into a greased and base-lined 18 cm (7 in) round cake tin and bake in a very moderate oven, 160°C (325°F) Gas Mark 3 for 65 minutes or until the cake is resilient to the touch. Turn out on to a wire rack, remove the paper and leave until cold.

To make the icing put all the ingredients into the processor bowl and mix until smooth and well blended. Split the cake in half and sandwich with half the icing; spread the remainder over the top of the cake.

Serves 8

SAUTÉED MUSHROOMS

Mushrooms should always be used when they are fresh, should never be washed and only be peeled if the skin is considerably discoloured. To clean wipe the smooth side of the mushrooms with a clean well squeezed out damp cloth. Sautéed mushrooms can be stored in the freezer and can then be used either defrosted or from their frozen state.

> 75 g (3 oz) butter
> Salt
> Pepper
> 450 g (1 lb) button mushrooms, wiped and thickly sliced (page 62)
> 5 ml (1tsp) lemon juice

Heat the butter in a shallow frying pan, add salt and pepper, the sliced mushrooms and the lemon juice and cook briskly until all the liquid has evaporated and the mushrooms are golden brown. Leave to cool, then spread the sliced mushrooms in even layers on sheets of foil or baking tins and open freeze. When frozen the mushrooms may be packed into freezer cartons.

Makes about 225 g (½ lb)

SCRAMBLED EGGS MORNAY

Single cream, Gouda cheese and freshly chopped chives make this recipe worthy of a better name. Serve as a light supper dish or for Sunday brunch. The dish can be made more substantial by serving with a helping of mashed potato.

> 8 eggs   METAL BLADE
> 60 ml (4 tbsp) single cream
> Shake Cayenne pepper
> Shake salt
> 25 g (1 oz) softened butter or soft margarine
> 100 g (4 oz) grated Gouda cheese (page 44)

For garnish:
30 ml (2 tbsp) freshly chopped chives (page 57)

Put the eggs and cream into the processor bowl and add a shake of Cayenne and salt. Do not add too much salt as the cheese has quite a lot of flavour. Add the butter or margarine and about three-quarters of the cheese and process until well mixed. Pour the mixture into a saucepan and cook over the lowest possible heat, stirring constantly until the eggs are set but still very creamy. Serve on warm plates and sprinkle with the remaining cheese and the chives.

Serves 4 to 5

SESAME PRAWN TOASTS

Pekinese Chinese restaurants serve these as a hot snack or starter. When to be served with chopsticks they should be cut into bite-sized pieces. Fresh ginger root is obtainable at ethnic grocers and in the larger supermarkets. Frozen prawns should be thawed and patted dry before use or the mixture will be too wet.

2.5 cm (1 in) piece fresh ginger root,   METAL BLADE
   peeled
225 g (8 oz) peeled cooked prawns
2 spring onions, bulbs only
10 ml (2 tsp) cornflour
1 egg
15 ml (1 tbsp) dry sherry
Salt
Freshly ground black pepper
6 pieces sliced white bread, crusts removed
60 ml (4 tbsp) sesame seeds
Oil for deep frying

Roughly cut up the ginger, put into the processor bowl and process until finely chopped. Add the prawns and spring onions and process until the onion is finely chopped. Scrape down the sides of the bowl once. Switch on the motor and while it is running add the cornflour, egg and sherry through the feed tube. Season the mixture to taste with salt and pepper. Spread the paste liberally on one side of each slice of bread and cut into fingers. Put the sesame seeds on a plate or piece of greaseproof paper and press the paste side of the bread on to the seeds. Turn the bread the right side up and press the sesame seeds in with a round-bladed knife. Pour about 1 cm (½ in) oil into a large frying pan, place over the heat and when a haze appears slide nine or ten sesame toasts into the oil, sesame-seed-side down and fry for about 45 seconds or until golden brown. Turn the toasts over and cook until the other side is crisp. Remove with a slotted spoon and drain on kitchen paper. Add a little more oil, then fry the remaining toasts. Serve hot.

Makes 18 to 24

SIMPLE MOUSSAKA

To prevent discolouration of the sliced potatoes, place them in a bowl of cold water covered tightly with clingfilm until required. Keep in the refrigerator for not more than 12 hours.

50 g (2 oz) butter or margarine
450 g (1 lb) potatoes, peeled and sliced (page 69)
350 g (12 oz) lean minced beef (page 61)
1 medium onion, chopped (page 63)
45 ml (3 tbsp) tomato purée
Salt
Pepper

450 ml (¾ pt) Béchamel sauce (page 166)
25 g (1 oz) grated Cheddar cheese (page 44)
25 g (1 oz) fresh breadcrumbs (page 36)

Heat the butter or margarine in a large frying pan, add the potatoes and sauté gently until just tender. Thinly sliced potatoes prepared in the food processor tend to stick together, so use tongs to separate the pieces while frying. Remove the cooked potatoes from the frying pan using a slotted spoon, raise the heat under the pan and add the meat and onion in small quantities. If you add too much at one time the temperature of the fat reduces and the meat stews rather than fries. Stir the meat and onion until browned, then add the tomato purée and season to taste with salt and pepper. Layer the potatoes and the meat in a casserole finishing with a layer of potatoes. Pour the sauce over the top and sprinkle with the grated cheese and breadcrumbs. Bake uncovered in a moderately hot oven, 190°C (375°F) Gas Mark 5, for 45 minutes to 1 hour or until the meat is cooked and the moussaka is brown on top.

Serves 4

SPAGHETTI PIEDMONTE

Although usually served with spaghetti the sauce is suitable to serve with all types of pasta.

15 g (½ oz) butter
15 ml (1 tbsp) oil
1 medium onion, peeled and finely chopped (page 63)
225 g (8 oz) veal, trimmed and finely chopped (page 61)

100 g (4 oz) chicken livers, rinsed, dried and trimmed
  of all sinews (page 45)
1 × 398 g (14 oz) can tomatoes
15 ml (1 tbsp) tomato purée
5 ml (1 tsp) fresh lemon juice
2.5 ml (½ tsp) dried oregano
Salt
Pepper
100 g (4 oz) spaghetti per person
15 ml (1 tbsp) cornflour

Heat the butter and oil in a large saucepan (preferably non-stick) and sauté the onion until just beginning to colour. Add the veal, a handful at a time and fry briskly, stirring continuously until the meat is brown. Stir in the chicken livers and cook until they are opaque, about 2 minutes. Add 150 ml (¼ pt) hot water, the contents of the can of tomatoes, the tomato purée, lemon juice, oregano and salt and pepper. Bring the sauce to the boil, then cover, reduce the heat and simmer for 30 minutes or until the mixture thickens.

Cook the spaghetti according to the instructions on the packet, adding a teaspoon of vegetable oil to the boiling salted water. Pasta cooking times vary considerably according to how thick the strands are, but it is unlikely to be less than 5 minutes and probably not more than 10 minutes. Drain thoroughly.

Blend the cornflour with 2 or 3 tablespoons cold water and stir into the sauce. Cook, stirring constantly, for 2 to 3 minutes to thicken the sauce and blend the flavours together.

Serve the spaghetti on a large dish or on separate hot plates, topped with the hot sauce.

The sauce serves 4 to 6

STUFFED BAKED AVOCADOS

The best avocado to buy is the one that is ripe. Avocados
that are slightly firm can be ripened in the airing cupboard
or at room temperature in a polythene bag, nestling close
to a banana for about 24 hours. But if the avocado is hard
hard then I find that they take days and days to ripen and
sometimes they are blackened inside.

2 slices ready-cut white bread,   METAL BLADE
   crusts removed
8 fresh chives, washed and dried
10 ml (2 tbsp) fresh lemon juice
30 ml (2 tbsp) mayonnaise (page 127)
30 ml (2 tbsp) soured cream
1 × 150 g (6 oz) can crabmeat, drained
Salt
Pepper
4 medium avocados
10 ml (2 tsp) grated Parmesan cheese (page 64)
10 ml (2 tsp) butter

Switch on the machine and add the bread, torn into
pieces, through the feed tube. As soon as the bread is
crumbed add the chives and when these are thoroughly
chopped, open the lid and add the lemon juice, mayonnaise, soured cream and crabmeat. Pulse once or twice to
mix the ingredients but not long enough to turn the
mixture into a smooth pâté. Season with salt and pepper.

Halve the avocados horizontally and remove the stones,
then pile the mixture into the cavities and sprinkle with the
cheese. Top with a dab of butter and bake without covering
in an oven-proof dish in a fairly hot oven, 200°C (400°F)
Gas Mark 6, for 20 to 25 minutes or until the avocado flesh
is tender and the cheese topping is browned.

Serves 4 to 8

STUFFED SPANISH ONIONS

Choose medium rather than outsize onions and if you find
that you have too much filling then bind the remainder
with a little beaten egg, form the mixture into balls and
bake on a greased baking sheet in the lower part of the
oven while the onions are cooking.

4 modest-sized Spanish onions   METAL BLADE
100 g (4 oz) breadcrumbs (page 36)
225 g (8 oz) lean ham, finely chopped (page 56)
30 ml (2 tbsp) single cream
Salt
Pepper
25 g (1 oz) butter or margarine

Peel the onions and place in a large pan of salted water.
Bring to the boil, then simmer for 20 to 30 minutes until
the onions are cooked but still firm. Remove the onions
with a slotted spoon and set aside. Reserve about 60 ml
(4 tbsp) of the cooking liquid and set the remainder aside
for making soups. Using a grapefruit knife, remove the
centres of the onions, leaving a 1 cm (½ in) thick wall. Put
the onion centres in the processor bowl and process until
finely chopped. Remove the lid and add the crumbs, ham,
cream and reserved juices and season with salt and
pepper. Process briefly to mix. Stuff the onions with the
mixture, put into a well greased oven-proof casserole and
dot the tops with the butter or margarine. Bake in a
moderately hot oven, 190°C (375°F) Gas Mark 5, for 25 to
35 minutes or until the outsides of the onions are tender
and golden.

Serves 4

TOMATO AND ONION SALAD

When you are making salads in large quantities, using your food processor will cut the preparation time considerably. To prevent tomatoes from squashing, process them in two or more lots, emptying the processor bowl as soon as it is full. Double up the recipe as many times as you require.

8 very small tomatoes, washed and dried and sliced (page 78)
1 very small onion, peeled and thinly sliced (page 63)
3 tbsp vinaigrette dressing (page 112)

Combine the sliced tomatoes and onion in a salad bowl. Cover and leave until required, then pour the well-shaken vinaigrette over the salad.

Serves 6

TOMATOES EN GELÉE

Choose brightly coloured tomatoes of uniform shape for this summer buffet dish or starter. If aspic crystals are not obtainable use powdered gelatine: Dissolve 1 level tsp gelatine powder in 1 tbsp hot water, add 4 fl oz cold water, 1 tsp lemon juice, 1 tbsp white vinegar, 1 tbsp caster sugar and a pinch of salt. Stir until the sugar is dissolved and leave until cool but not set.

16 small firm tomatoes, stalks removed   METAL BLADE
100 ml (4 fl oz) double cream
200 ml (8 fl oz) mayonnaise (page 127)
1 × 150 g (5 oz) can tomato purée

100 g (4 fl oz) aspic jelly (made up according to
    packet instructions)
15 ml (1 tbsp) finely chopped fresh basil leaves (page
    57) or 10 ml (2 tsp) dried basil
1.25 ml (¼ tsp) garlic salt
1.25 ml (¼ tsp) pepper

For garnishing:
Freshly washed endive leaves

Remove a slice from the top of each tomato and set aside.
Scoop out the tomato pulp and remove the pips. Sprinkle
the tomato cavities with salt. Turn the tomato shells
upside-down to drain. Switch on the machine and while
the motor is running, pour in the cream rapidly through
the feed tube and process until it thickens. Add the
mayonnaise, tomato purée, cooled but not set aspic jelly,
basil, garlic salt, pepper and the reserved tomato pulp.
Process the mixture to a smooth cream, scraping down the
sides of the bowl once. Taste and adjust the seasoning if
necessary. Spoon the purée into the tomato shells and
refrigerate for 2 to 3 hours or until the mixture is set. Place
the filled tomatoes on a bed of endive leaves. This will
help to keep the tomatoes upright. Balance the lids on
top.

Serves 8 to 16

TURKEY TOPPER

Left-over turkey can be used up in all sorts of dishes. In
this recipe it is cooked with the other ingredients to make
a thick topping that can be served on toast or over cooked
boiled rice or even creamed potatoes.

350 g (12 oz) cold cooked turkey, roughly chopped
   (page 70)
100 g (4 oz) butter or margarine
1 medium onion, peeled and chopped (page 63)
3 rashers lean bacon, derinded and chopped (page
   32)
30 ml (2 tbsp) plain flour
50 g (2 oz) mushrooms, sliced (page 62)
300 ml (½ pt) turkey stock
15 ml (1 tbsp) tomato purée
60 ml (4 tbsp) sherry
Salt
Pepper

Sauté the turkey in half the butter or margarine in a large
pan for about 5 minutes or until the turkey is thoroughly
heated. Remove the turkey with a slotted spoon, cover
and keep hot. Stir the onion and bacon into the juices in
the pan, add the remaining butter and cook gently until
the bacon and onion are soft. Stir in the flour and the
mushrooms and cook for 1 minute, then mix in the stock,
tomato purée, sherry and seasoning. Simmer for 5 minutes, stirring continuously. Then taste and adjust the
seasoning. Quickly mix in the turkey and serve at once.
This dish should not be reheated.

Serves 4 to 6

UNSOPHISTICATED LAMB CURRY

Curries are becoming more and more popular and many
of us buy take-aways from the local Indian restaurant, but
there are still huge numbers of people who prefer the
ordinary English-type curry and this recipe is for them.

1 large onion, peeled and chopped (page 63)
1 stick celery, chopped (page 43)
30 ml (2 tbsp) vegetable oil
100 g (4 oz) mushrooms, sliced (page 62)
30 ml (2 tbsp) flour
15 ml (1 tbsp) curry powder
15 ml (1 tbsp) tomato purée
30 ml (1 rounded tbsp) mango chutney
600 ml (1 pt) hot stock
450 g (1 lb) cooked lamb, coarsely chopped (page 61)
50 g (2 oz) sultanas
Salt
30 ml (2 tbsp) natural yoghurt

Sauté the onion and celery in the oil in a large saucepan, then stir in the mushrooms and cook for 2 minutes. Add the flour, curry powder, tomato purée and mango chutney and stir thoroughly, then gradually mix in the stock. Bring to the boil, stirring continuously until the mixture thickens, then add the chopped meat and sultanas. Add salt to taste but do not over-season as the curry becomes saltier during cooking. Cover with the lid and simmer for 30 to 45 minutes, then stir in the yoghurt and serve hot. Do not reheat after the yoghurt has been added. If you are not serving the dish at once, stir a teaspoon of cornflour into the yoghurt before adding to the curry, then bring to the boil. Serve with boiled rice and sliced tomatoes and onions mixed together and topped with paprika.

Serves 4

YORKSHIRE CORACLES

When Yorkshire pudding batter is baked in individual bun tins the mixture often rises around the sides leaving a dip in the middle. This can then be filled with any sweet or savoury stuffing. This recipe is for a light supper dish. The batter can be prepared up to 12 hours ahead and stored in the refrigerator.

100 g (4 oz) plain flour   METAL BLADE
Pinch salt
2 size-2 eggs
300 ml (½ pt) milk

For the filling:
2 × 225 g (8 oz) cans chicken pieces in white sauce
75 g (3 oz) grated Cheddar cheese (page 44)
Vegetable oil for greasing

To prepare the batter, first put the flour, salt and eggs in the processor bowl and add about half the milk. Process until smooth, then while the machine is still running, add the remainder of the milk through the feed tube. Scrape down the sides of the bowl, then process to a thin smooth batter. Pour into a jug and leave in a cool place for 30 minutes before using. While the batter is standing, prepare the filling and set the oven to hot, 220°C (425°F) Gas Mark 7.

To prepare the filling, just empty the cans of chicken into a saucepan and heat gently until the mixture can be easily stirred. Remove from the heat and mix in half the cheese.

Put a teaspoon of oil into each of twelve or fifteen patty tins and place in the oven. When the oil begins to smoke, three-quarters fill each tin with batter. Bake in the top part of the oven for 15 to 20 minutes or until the puddings are well risen, brown and crisp on top. Remove the tins from the oven and loosen the puddings with a grapefruit knife. Press down the centres and spoon the filling into the wells. Sprinkle with the remaining cheese, then replace the tins in the oven until the cheese melts. Serve immediately.

Makes 12 to 15, serves 6

FAST FOOD

The food processor speeds preparation. The microwave oven and the pressure cooker speed cooking. Use them in conjunction for the fastest dishes ever.

To get the best out of the microwave the food should be evenly shaped. This is particularly important when cooking vegetables.

Pressure- or microwave-cooked foods can be puréed in the food processor in seconds, and steamed puddings mixed quickly in the food processor take just a few minutes to cook. The pressure cooker is best for tenderizing meat, cooking pulses and for when moist cooking is required. The microwave oven is neither a wet nor dry type of cooking and so is more versatile as it can carry out many of the processes normally done on the hob or in the oven. It cannot take the place of a grill or be used for deep frying. Both are excellent appliances – with the help of the food processor they are miraculous.

BACON AND LIVER TERRINE

This plain basic recipe is made more attractive by the garnish of golden crumbs.

100 g (4 oz) butter or margarine   METAL BLADE
100 g (4 oz) fresh breadcrumbs   MICROWAVE OVEN
350 g (12 oz) lean cooked bacon, cubed
100 g (4 oz) lamb's liver
1 medium onion, peeled
5 Dutch tea rusks or Cracotte biscuits, broken up
30 ml (2 tbsp) fresh parsley
1 size-3 egg
150 ml (¼ pt) milk
Salt
Pepper

Put the butter or margarine and the breadcrumbs into an oven-glass loaf dish or suitable casserole and microwave on full power for 6 to 7 minutes, stirring occasionally until the butter is absorbed and the breadcrumbs are a golden colour. Switch on the food processor and add the bacon, liver and the onion, cut into four pieces, through the feed tube and process until finely chopped. Remove the lid and add the rusks or biscuits, the parsley, egg and milk and season sparingly with salt and pepper. Process until the mixture is smooth. The mixture will be speckled with parsley. Scoop half the crumbs from the dish, then fill with the bacon mixture, pressing it down well. Spoon the reserved crumbs over the top and cover with greaseproof paper. The paper should not be bigger than the surface of the dish or it may blow off during cooking. Microwave on full power for 12 to 14 minutes, giving the dish a quarter-turn three times during cooking. Leave to stand for 10 minutes before serving either directly from the dish or turned out on to a heated serving platter.

Serves 4 to 6

BLACKBERRY PUD

A steamed pudding made from store cupboard ingredients. If you haven't any blackberries, substitute apricots, peaches or blackcurrants.

1 × 213 g (7½ oz) can blackberries,   METAL BLADE
   drained   PRESSURE COOKER
100 g x(4 oz) soft butter or margarine
100 g (4 oz) caster sugar
2 size-2 eggs
100 g (4 oz) self-raising flour
2.5 ml (½ tsp) baking powder
Pinch salt
15 ml (1 tbsp) milk

Well grease a 1.1 litre (2 pt) pudding basin and spoon the blackberries into the base. Put all the remaining ingredients into the processor bowl and process for 25 seconds or until smooth. Scrape down the sides of the bowl once during processing. Spoon the mixture over the blackberries and smooth the surface. Cover the basin with a double layer of greased greaseproof paper and tie securely with string.

To pressure cook, place the basin on the trivet in the pressure cooker which should contain about 700 ml (1¼ pt) boiling water and a teaspoon of vinegar or lemon juice. Steam for 15 minutes, then cook for 25 minutes at 5 lb pressure. Allow the pressure to reduce at room temperature, then turn out and serve in the usual way with custard or whipped cream.

Alternatively the pudding can be cooked for 2 hours in a steamer or large lidded saucepan half-filled with boiling water, adding more boiling water as necessary.

Serves 4

CHICKEN MAYONNAISE SALAD

Boned fresh chilled chicken breasts are obtainable at larger supermarkets. To cook quickly remove the skin, flatten with a cleaver, then cover and cook in the microwave oven. Four chicken breasts will take about 6 to 8 minutes. Leave to cool.

450 g (1 lb) cooked breast of chicken,   PLASTIC BLADE
   roughly chopped (page 70)
150 ml (¼ pt) mayonnaise (page 127)
150 ml (¼ pt) natural yoghurt
15 ml (1 tbsp) curry powder
Salt
Pepper
Lettuce leaves
6 stoned black olives, finely chopped (page 63)
2 hard-boiled eggs, roughly chopped (page 53)
1 sweet and sour pickled cucumber, sliced (page 52)
6 stoned green olives, finely chopped (page 63)

Thoroughly mix the chicken, mayonnaise, yoghurt and curry powder together either in the processor bowl or a mixing bowl. Season to taste with salt and pepper. Arrange the lettuce leaves on individual serving dishes or a larger dish and spoon the chicken mixture on top. Garnish with well-defined lines of chopped black olives, eggs, sliced cucumber, chopped green olives (in that order).

Serves 4

CHRISTMAS PUDDING

This dark soft moist pudding takes about 30 minutes to cook but it is improved if the fruit is soaked overnight. The pudding improves with keeping.

¼ cooking apple, peeled, cored and   METAL BLADE
   quartered   MICROWAVE OVEN
15 g (½ oz) blanched almonds
75 ml (5 tbsp) medium sherry
45 ml (3 tbsp) brandy
1.25 ml (¼ tsp) ground nutmeg
1.25 ml (¼ tsp) ground mixed spice
5 ml (1 tsp) lemon juice
15 ml (1 tbsp) black treacle
100 g (4 oz) muscovado sugar
75 g (3 oz) butter
75 g (3 oz) crumbs from a fresh granary loaf
25 g (1 oz) plain flour
2 size-3 eggs
100 g (4 oz) currants
100 g (4 oz) sultanas
100 g (4 oz) seedless raisins

Switch on the machine and process the apple and nuts until finely chopped. Then add the remaining ingredients except the dried fruit in the order given. (If the mixture is too much for the processor bowl, the ingredients may be processed in batches, then combined in a large mixing bowl.) Turn the mixture into a large mixing bowl and stir in the dried fruit. Well grease a 1.1 litre (2 pt) oven-glass pudding basin and place a 5 cm (2 in) disc of non-stick paper in the base. Spoon the mixture into the basin and cover loosely with clingfilm. Leave overnight. The next day pull back one corner of the clingfilm so that the pudding is vented, place in the microwave oven and microwave on the defrost setting (about 35 per cent of full power) for about 30 minutes. Cook only until the pudding is just dry on top, then leave until cold before turning out. Pour over one or two more tablespoons of brandy, wrap the pudding in clingfilm and cover with foil if not using immediately. To reheat, remove the wrapping and put the pudding in a greased pudding basin or other suitable dish and place in the microwave oven, allowing 3 to 5 minutes cooking time depending upon the power of your oven.

Serves 5 to 6

COUNTRY-STYLE CHICKEN

Skin the chicken before casseroling by microwave and then you will have a non-greasy ready-to-serve meal. Use either the casserole lid or vented clingfilm to cover.

225 g (8 oz) white part of leeks   SLICING DISC
2 celery stalks   MICROWAVE OVEN
350 g (12 oz) large potatoes, peeled and cut into
    quarters
2 carrots, peeled
450 ml (¾ pt) boiling chicken stock
2.5 ml (½ tsp) paprika
1.5 kg (3½ lb) skinned chicken joints
1 × 398 g (14 oz) can tomatoes
Salt
Pepper

Attach the slicing disc and process the vegetables. Put the sliced vegetables in a suitable large casserole and add the boiling stock. Stir once, then cover and microwave on full power for 5 minutes, stirring once during cooking. Rub the paprika over the chicken joints and arrange them in the casserole. Add the canned tomatoes and their juice, then season sparingly with salt and pepper. Cover and microwave on full power for 25 to 35 minutes, repositioning the chicken twice during cooking. Leave to stand, covered, for 15 minutes before serving.

Serves 4 to 5

HAM AND PEA SOUP

30 seconds to process and 8 minutes to cook seems a ridiculously short time for such a lovely soup.

15 ml (1 tbsp) sautéed onion purée (page 194)	METAL BLADE
	MICROWAVE OVEN

1 × 539 g (1 lb 3 oz) can processed peas
1 chicken stock cube, crumbled
75 g (3 oz) ham
200 ml (7 fl oz) milk
Salt
Pepper
60 ml (4 tbsp) double cream

For garnish:
Browned crumbs (page 36)

Put the sautéed onion purée and the contents of the can of peas, the stock cube and ham in the processor bowl and process until smooth. Scrape down the sides of the bowl once. Pour into a large microwave-proof bowl and stir in the milk. Three-quarters cover with clingfilm and microwave on full power for 8 minutes. Stir occasionally through the gap in the clingfilm during cooking. Add salt sparingly and pepper to taste. Stir in the cream then pour the soup into individual bowls and garnish each with browned crumbs.

Serves 4; makes 700 ml (1¼ pt)

LEMON CURD

Lemon curd mixture is easy to prepare in the food processor but when made conventionally, has to be

cooked in a double saucepan. If you use the microwave
oven you will have successful lemon curd in no time at all.

Juice and grated rind of two   METAL BLADE
   large lemons   MICROWAVE OVEN
100 g (4 oz) unsalted butter, softened
225 g (8 oz) granulated sugar
2 size-2 eggs

Put all the ingredients into the processor bowl and process
until the sugar begins to dissolve. This may look curdled
but is all right. Pour the mixture into an oven-glass mixing
bowl, place in the microwave oven and cook on full power
for 2 to 3 minutes, whisking every 30 seconds until the
curd thickens sufficiently to coat the back of a wooden
spoon. Pour into sterilized jars and cover in the usual way.

Makes 1 to 1½ jam jars

LYONNAISE POTATOES

This is one of my favourite never-fail microwave recipes
but you must make sure that you use a flame-proof dish so
that the top can be browned under the grill.

1 medium onion, peeled and finely   METAL BLADE
   chopped (page 63)   THIN SLICING DISC
20 g (¾ oz) butter or margarine   MICROWAVE OVEN
60 ml (4 tbsp) double cream
450 g (1 lb) old potatoes, peeled and thinly sliced
   (page 69)
Salt
Pepper

Put the onion and the butter or margarine in a 23 cm (9 in)
round shallow flame-proof dish and microwave on full

power for 3 to 4 minutes until the onion is soft. Stir every minute, so that the onion and butter are well mixed. Stir in the cream, then add the potatoes a few at a time, seasoning with salt and pepper and turning the slices over so that they are well coated with the butter mixture. Cover the dish with clingfilm and pull back one corner to vent. Microwave on full power for 10 to 12 minutes or until the potatoes are tender. Leave for 5 minutes, then carefully remove the clingfilm and brown the potatoes under the grill.

Serves 4

PRAWN AND ASPARAGUS PANCAKES

Make up a batch of pancakes whenever you have time, then layer them between sheets of greaseproof paper and place in a polythene bag. To store for more than a few hours, seal well and freeze. Thaw before using. To defrost, remove the stack of pancakes from the polythene bag and place together with the interleaving paper in the microwave oven set on defrost. Switch off the power when the pancake edges are pliable.

1 × 340 g (12 oz) can asparagus tips   METAL BLADE
25 g (1 oz) butter or margarine   MICROWAVE OVEN
25 g (1 oz) flour
150 ml (¼ pt) milk
150 ml (¼ pt) single cream
175 g (6 oz) cooked shelled prawns
8 pancakes
60 ml (4 tbsp) grated Cheddar cheese (page 44)

Drain the asparagus and place in the processor bowl with the butter or margarine, flour, milk and cream. Insert the pusher in the feed tube and process until the mixture is blended. The butter will not melt at this stage but this is not important. Pour the mixture into a large microwave-proof bowl and microwave on full power for 5 minutes, whisking thoroughly every 2 minutes. Stir in the prawns.

Divide the mixture between the pancakes, then roll up and place the pancakes in a microwave-proof shallow dish. Sprinkle with the grated cheese, then microwave on full power for 1 minute or until the cheese has melted. Serve at once.

Serves 4 to 5

RASPBERRY CURD

Use fresh or frozen raspberries for this unusual spread which is delicious with tea breads or freshly made scones. Frozen raspberries should be thawed before using.

225 g (8 oz) raspberries   METAL BLADE
100 g (4 oz) caster sugar   MICROWAVE OVEN
2 size-2 eggs plus 2 yolks
50 g (2 oz) butter

Put the raspberries and sugar in the processor bowl and process to a purée. While the machine is running add the eggs and the extra yolks through the feed tube and blend thoroughly. Put the butter in a 1.95 litre (3½ pt) microwave-proof bowl and microwave on full power for 30 seconds to 1 minute until melted. Stir in the raspberry mixture and microwave on full power for 4 minutes, whisking every 30 seconds until the curd thickens. Remove from the microwave oven and press through a nylon sieve into a cool bowl if you wish to remove the pips. Beat the curd vigorously for a few minutes. For same-day serving pour the curd into a bowl and refrigerate until cold. The curd may be potted in the same way as jam and will keep in the refrigerator for 2 to 3 weeks.

Makes 450 g (1 lb)

RASPBERRY ICE CREAM

Substitute strawberries, loganberries or blackberries to ring the changes. There is no need to rinse the processor bowl before thickening the cream.

450 g (1 lb) raspberries, fresh or thawed METAL BLADE
30 ml (2 tbsp) lemon juice   MICROWAVE OVEN
150 g (5 oz) caster sugar
300 ml (½ pt) double cream

Put the raspberries in the processor bowl with the lemon juice and process until puréed. Press the purée through a sieve to remove the pips. Combine the sugar and 90 ml (6 tbsp) water in a large oven-glass bowl, and microwave on full power for 1 minute or until the sugar has dissolved. Stir thoroughly, then microwave on full power until the syrup boils and continue boiling for 1 to 2 minutes until the syrup thickens but does not colour. The process should not take more than 5 minutes from start to finish. Leave to cool.

Switch on the food processor and quickly pour in the cream through the feed tube while the motor is running, and process until the cream thickens. Remove the lid, add the puréed raspberries and the cooled syrup and pulse until the mixture is an even colour. Spoon into an ice-cube tray and freeze for about 2 hours until partly frozen. Scoop the mixture into the processor bowl and process until well mixed, then return the mixture to the ice tray and freeze until solid. Transfer to the refrigerator 5 minutes before serving.

Serves 6 to 8; makes 900 ml (1½ pt)

SCALLOPS IN SAFFRON, LEMON AND GARLIC SAUCE

This is an excellent dinner-party starter or light supper dish which may be served with boiled rice. Serve in scallop shells garnished with a thin slice of lemon. Make up the sauce at a convenient time, up to 2 days ahead, and store (covered) in the refrigerator. Cook the scallops in the sauce in a casserole dish using the defrost setting on your microwave oven. The sauce is also excellent with any white fish fillets or cutlets.

600 ml (1 pt) milk	METAL BLADE
50 g (2 oz) flour	MICROWAVE OVEN
50 g (2 oz) butter or margarine	
1.25 ml (¼ tsp) saffron powder	
45 ml (3 tbsp) fresh lemon juice	
1 clove garlic, crushed	
Salt	
Pepper	
450 g (1 lb) frozen scallops, thawed or 6 large	
scallops, halved	

For garnish:
Lemon slices

Pour the milk into a 1.1 litre (2 pt) lipped microwave-proof bowl and microwave on full power for 4 minutes or until the milk begins to boil. Meanwhile put the flour and butter or margarine in the processor bowl and process until the mixture forms a paste. When the milk is ready, switch on the food processor and pour the milk into the butter paste through the feed tube. Process until smooth, scraping down the sides of the bowl once. Add the saffron powder, lemon juice and garlic and process briefly to mix, then season to taste with salt and pepper. Return the mixture to the cooking bowl and microwave on full power for 3 minutes, beating every minute with a wire whisk. Add the scallops, making sure that the coral is pierced to prevent it bursting. Reduce the setting to low or defrost (35 per cent full power) and microwave for 10 to 14 minutes, stirring occasionally, or until cooked. Divide the scallops between four or six shells, spoon the sauce over the top and garnish with a slice of lemon.

Serves 4 to 6

STEAK AND KIDNEY PUDDING

When the meat is chopped in the food processor the cooking time is greatly reduced, particularly if you are accustomed to cooking the filling before putting it into the pastry. Cooking this recipe by microwave will shorten the cooking time even more. If you prefer to prepare the filling by microwave and then cook the pudding in a pressure cooker, give 10 minutes' steaming followed by 35 minutes at 5 lb pressure. The filling will take 15 minutes at 15 lb pressure in the pressure cooker.

2 onions, peeled	METAL BLADE
225 g (8 oz) ox kidney	MICROWAVE OVEN *or*
450 g (1 lb) lean beef	PRESSURE COOKER
25 g (1 oz) butter	
25 g (1 oz) flour	
200 ml (⅓ pt) hot water	
1 beef stock cube, crumbled	

5 ml (1 tsp) salt
1.25 ml (¼ tsp) black pepper

Pastry:
225 g (8 oz) plain flour
10 ml (2 tsp) baking powder
5 ml (1 tsp) salt
100 g (4 oz) shredded suet
8 to 10 tbsp cold water

Cut the onions into chunks. Wash the kidney under cold running water, remove the core and roughly chop the kidney. Cut the meat into 2.5 cm (1 in) cubes. Switch on the machine and drop the onion pieces through the feed tube and process until finely chopped. Remove the lid, put half the meat cubes in the processor bowl, then pulse until roughly chopped but not minced. Remove the chopped meat from the bowl, then process the remaining meat together with the kidney, pulsing until roughly chopped. Put the butter in a non-metallic deep casserole and microwave on full power for 45 seconds or until melted. Blend in the flour, then stir in the water and all the other ingredients. Cover with the lid and microwave on full power for 20 minutes, stirring occasionally. Reduce the setting and microwave on low or defrost for 15 minutes, stirring occasionally.

To make the pastry, first rinse and dry the processor bowl thoroughly. Then put the flour, baking powder and salt into the bowl and process for 2 or 3 seconds. Remove the lid and add the suet, sprinkling it evenly on top of the flour mixture, then switch on the machine and add the water through the feed tube while the motor is running. Add only sufficient water to mix to a soft dough, which should just leave the sides of the bowl. Remove the pastry from the bowl and shape into a ball on a floured surface. Set aside one-quarter of the pastry and roll the remainder to fit into a 1 litre (1¾ pt) pudding basin. Fill with the steak and kidney mixture and fold the surplus pastry over the filling. Brush the folded-over pastry with water. Roll out the reserved pastry to form a lid and place on the top, pressing the edges together to seal. Slit the pastry lid two or three times with a sharp knife. Cover the pastry very loosely with clingfilm (you will require double the length normally used to allow for expansion). Microwave on low or defrost for 15 minutes, giving the pudding basin a half-turn three or four times during cooking. At the end of the cooking time, leave the pudding to stand for 10 minutes before serving.

Serves 4 to 6

List of Manufacturers

To make the book as comprehensive as possible and to ensure that the recipes and glossary instructions are as foolproof as possible, a wide range of different food processors was used. Included among the manufacturers are:

BRAUN
Braun Electric (UK) Ltd, Dolphin Estate, Windmill Road, Sunbury-on-Thames, Middx.

BREVILLE
Breville Europe Ltd, Alexandra House, Alexandra Terrace, Guildford, Surrey, GU1 3DA.

IONA
General Signal Appliances Ltd, Dominion Way, Worthing, Sussex, BN14, 8NW.

KENWOOD
Thorn EMI Domestic Electrical Appliances Ltd, New Lane, Havant, Hants, PO9 2NH.

MAGIMIX
ICTC Electrical Ltd, 632/652 London Road, Isleworth, Middx, TW7 4EZ.

MOULINEX
Moulinex Ltd, Station Approach, Coulsdon North, Coulsdon, Surrey, CR2 2UD.

PRESTIGE
The Prestige Group plc, Prestige House, 14/18 Holborn, London, EC1N 2LQ.

TOSHIBA
Toshiba (UK) Ltd, Toshiba House, Frimley Road, Frimley, Camberley, Surrey, GU16 5JJ.

Index